Twentysomething

Lawrence J. Bradford, Ph.D.,
and Claire Raines, M.A.
with Jo Leda Martin

Twentysomething

Managing and Motivating
Today's New Workforce

Merrill-Alexander Publishing, Denver

Merrill-Alexander Publishing

Library of Congress Cataloging-in-Publication Data
Bradford, Lawrence J.
    Twentysomething : managing and motivating today's new workforce / Lawrence J. Bradford and Claire Raines with Jo Leda Martin.
        p.   cm.
    Includes bibliographical references.
    ISBN 0-942361-35-0
    1. Supervision of employees. 2. Employee motivation. I. Raines, Claire. II. Martin, Jo Leda. III. Title. IV. Title: Twentysomething.
    HF5549.12.B73 1992
    658.3'02—dc20   91-60814
                                                          CIP

Designed by Jackie Schuman
Manufactured in the United States of America
10 9 8 7 6 5 4 3

Contents

Foreword   *ix*

Introduction   *xi*

1. Meet the Twentysomething Generation   *1*

2. When Manager and Worker Don't See Eye-to-Eye   *20*

3. Does Anything Matter to Them?   *31*

4. The Rainbow Coalition at Work   *52*

5. Workforce 2000: A Report Card   *68*

6. What Managers and Workers Are Saying   *85*

7. How to Resist an Overwhelming Urge to Choke the Living Daylights Out of Some Young Hotshot Who Desperately Needs It   *101*

8. Flexi-Leadership: A New Skill for the 1990s   *124*

9. How to Help Young Supervisors Avoid the Yellow Sneaker Syndrome   *145*

10. Here Today, Gone Tomorrow: Temporary and Seasonal Workers   *165*

11. Letter to a Manager   *177*

12. It's Up to You   *195*

It's hard to chase the baby boomers,
who have so much and left us so dry.
Patty, age twenty-four

Acknowledgments

For three years, Jim Ring, human resources manager for the Business Services Group of ARA Services, encouraged us, loaned his videotapes, and referred contacts.

Bill Hill, management professor at Colorado Mountain College in Steamboat Springs, Colorado, seems to be the national expert on temporary and seasonal workers. His help in this area was tremendously valuable.

A couple of years ago, when we decided to pursue the twentysomething topic seriously, Linda Keller, a poet and artist from Denver, spent days in the library looking for information. At that time, almost nothing had been written, even in magazines and daily papers. Linda's task was often frustrating.

Coleen Hubbard, a playwright and author from Denver, contributed significantly by researching and writing sections of some of the chapters. We are grateful for her ability to pick up our purpose and style instantly and produce what we needed.

Chris Levy, who directs The Executive Connection in Australia, read the manuscript from cover to cover and offered many helpful suggestions.

Finally, we offer our thanks to clients we've consulted and participants we've trained. Your insights, examples, and excitement got us started, kept us going, and contributed significantly to the pages that follow.

Foreword

I believe America is coming into a period of crisis. It's a crisis of many dimensions. Never before have Americans been so unsure of The American Way—so confused about what's real, what counts, and what to do with their lives.

One of the many dimensions of this crisis is a crisis in job, career, and personal direction. We have a whole generation of very troubled young people coming into the workforce, and it will be our challenge to help them deal with their troubles and find meaning in their lives. I will go so far as to say we must literally reclaim a lost generation.

Today's children, adolescents, and teenagers are without doubt the most commercially exploited generation in our history. They are richer, better fed, better dressed, more indulged, more confused about who they are, more cynical, and less committed to anything than any generation has ever been.

In many ways they are the most cheated generation that has ever come along. The American high-pressure video culture of hedonistic immediacy has robbed them of their childhood and made them into decadent, worldly mini-adults. It has taken from them the opportunity to learn the most basic human values of honesty, self-restraint, consideration for others, playing by the rules, and hard work. And now they come to us in all their diversity and varying degrees of maturity and commitment to ethical values.

If the leaders of American organizations, in both public and private sectors, hope to build strong, vibrant cultures based on a commitment to service and quality, they will have to grow and develop these mini-adults into competent, committed workers and organizational citizens. The challenge is enormous, and it will not go away.

I am optimistic that our leaders will face up to the challenge, although it will surely be a very stressful adaptation for both the leaders and the led.

Larry Bradford and Claire Raines have done a great job of defining this new workforce, and they have given us workable methods and techniques for motivating and managing them. They explain who these folks are, how they got that way, and what we must do to develop them into valuable contributors to our organizations. *Twentysomething* makes a much-needed contribution in an area which is vital to the success of American business.

—Karl Albrecht,
co-author of *Service America!* and
author of *The Only Thing That Matters*

Introduction

Have you ever heard yourself say, "You just can't get good help anymore"? Try this one on for size: "You can't get *any* help anymore!" The pool of entry-level workers in the United States today is smaller than at any time in the past fifty years. Also, the workers who are going to be available in the next few years are an entirely different breed of feline.

If you're a manager today, it's because you've put in years doing lots of hard work to get where you are. But young employees in this last decade of the twentieth century have very different values and assumptions about work and "the job" than you do. They want what they want, and they want it *now*. They're not particularly respectful of authority, tend to ignore chains of command, believe hierarchies are irrelevant, and aren't put off by the threat of being fired. At the same time, they possess a tremendous driving force, which pushes them toward accomplishing their goals. They bring energy, innovation, and a willingness to challenge systems unlike any other generation. They're small in number, but mighty in the impact they will have on American business.

If you're supervising employees between the ages of seventeen and twenty-seven, this book is for you. If you're frustrated in your efforts to understand this new generation, then you need to read this book now. If nothing else, it may help you to override that occasionally overwhelming urge to choke the living daylights out of some young hotshot who desperately needs it.

Why This Book?

If you're standing in a bookstore at this moment, take a look around at the business books at hand. We'll wager you won't see very many dealing with managing and motivating younger workers, because the attention in the past few years has been focused on the largest population of American workers and managers—the generation born between 1946 and 1964. If you're among them, then you're one of 76 million baby boomers, and thousands of pages in hundreds of books have been devoted to understanding your generation. But very little has been written to help your generation, and the one before you, understand and motivate the newest generation, the baby busters.

What we've discovered, in speaking to managers throughout the United States, is a highly frustrated and visibly angry group of baby boomers who are faced with managing a new generation. We've also encountered a sizable number of frustrated pre-baby boomers—the generation we call the loyalists. They're the folks born between 1925 and 1945, who are now in senior management and executive positions. Many of the older ones are entering retirement.

From both groups we hear a common theme when today's managers talk about today's entry-level workers:

"He wants everything without earning it."

"They don't have any respect for authority."

"She just goes right past me and ignores the fact that I'm her boss!"

"Why does he have to know 'why?' every time I tell him to do something?"

Sound familiar? Katherine Ann Samon, in an article for *Working Woman* magazine, coined the phrase "The Brash Pack," when describing this new generation.[1] In many ways, they *are* brash. But, weren't we all when we first started out? Not in the same way as this twentysomething crowd. They're the product of a very different type of upbringing and, as a result, are driven by different motivations. It's critical that you understand what drives these young people because this is the generation that will supply us with the bulk of our employees for the next ten years. Attracting, hiring, motivating, and developing them will be *the* major challenge facing managers of the nineties.

Michael Maccoby, author of *Why Work: Motivating and Leading the New Generation,* believes that the baby busters are a product, to a great extent, of their growing-up years, many of which were spent in homes where both parents worked.[2] These are the latchkey children you've heard about. As we'll see in the chapters ahead, these latchkey children have developed some interesting and challenging attitudes about themselves and the way they want to work.

San Francisco writer Sophie F. Deprez reviewed the novel *Generation X* by Douglas Coupland for the *San Francisco Chronicle.* Coupland calls his characters "Generation X" and they are the twentysomething generation. Deprez writes:

> Disillusioned by yuppiedom—and the materialism, restriction and artificiality it represents—too old to accept the notion of shopping malls as vital structures, yet too progressive and sophisticated to regress to sheer hippie-ism, they have rejected their past and their future and have chosen to explore the many possibilities complete freedom offers.[3]

We can't promise that by reading this book all your problems in leading and motivating this younger generation will disappear. But we can promise that you'll gain new understanding and insight into their attitudes, beliefs, and values. You'll have an opportunity to read their own words as they describe what makes them tick. And you'll find plenty of practical suggestions for getting the greatest productivity from this very special group of workers.

No matter what we or anyone else may say, generations are going to continue to collide. As different world views clash, conflict between generations is inevitable. Our intention in writing this book is to ease the impact a bit, so the managers and workers involved can meet one another on some productive middle ground. We believe this is essential. We've asked a colleague of ours—herself a twentysomething worker—to write a message to all managers. You'll read an open letter from her in chapter eleven. Though understanding doesn't always mean that agreement will occur, it is a prerequisite in leading, motivating, and working with today's employees. That's what this book is all about.

Notes

1. Katherine Ann Samon, "The Brash Pack," *Working Woman,* August, 1990, p. 67.
2. Michael Maccoby, *Why Work: Motivating and Leading the New Generation,* Touchstone: New York, NY, 1988.
3. Sophie F. Deprez, "The Twentysomething Gang," *The San Francisco Chronicle,* April 14, 1991, p. 8.

*The younger generation is not going to the dogs
. . . but it's a very mixed kennel.*
—Former Education Secretary Chester Finn

1

Meet the Twentysomething Generation

We assume you're reading this book because you now manage, or expect to hire and manage, young workers between the ages of seventeen and twenty-seven. You want your employees to be as productive as possible. After all, the success of your business depends upon worker productivity. As a leader, you want to develop your subordinates to be the best they can be. To manage them effectively, you need to know something about them. The young adults of this new generation have some unique characteristics, ranging from their demographics to their skills and education, their attitudes toward work, their attitudes toward themselves and others, how they see the world, their drive toward independence, and how they respond to authority.

Maybe you're saying to yourself, "I know everything I need to know about them." We've heard quite a few managers voice that kind of sentiment with a decided note of exasperation. Take a few minutes to read the ten statements below and decide on a scale of one to five the extent to which you agree or disagree with each of them.

If you find yourself agreeing with most of these statements, you're not alone. These are but a few of the many complaints we've heard from managers all over the country when they talk about their

	Disagree →			Agree	
• Young workers today have a "you owe me" attitude.	1	2	3	4	5
• Young people are interested in making a lot of money fast.	1	2	3	4	5
• Young workers are well educated, but their skills are poor.	1	2	3	4	5
• Young workers are too impatient.	1	2	3	4	5
• Young workers don't want to work hard.	1	2	3	4	5
• They don't want to start at the bottom and work their way up.	1	2	3	4	5
• Younger workers have very little company loyalty.	1	2	3	4	5
• They complain a lot.	1	2	3	4	5
• Young workers aren't team players.	1	2	3	4	5
• They lack motivation.	1	2	3	4	5

younger employees. Most managers' scores are in the four-to-five range on all the above. We're not saying these statements are true or false, only that they are valid perceptions today's managers have formed about their employees.

The purpose of this chapter is to give you a snapshot of these young workers and lay a foundation for a better understanding of this group. Subsequent chapters will add detail, expand your knowledge, and pave the way for acquiring new skills in motivating and leading them. For starters, let's meet the twentysomething generation.

A Limited Edition

There's no doubt that young people entering the workforce today are a limited edition. These baby busters were born between 1965 and 1975. They get their name because they represent a decided drop in the birth curve when compared to all previous years, but especially the baby boom years of 1946 to 1964. The single lowest birth year in U.S. history was 1975. Young people born in that year will be seventeen in 1992 and can expect to begin their professional careers by about 1997, if you allow a few years for college (although not all of them will take the mortarboard route).

As the smallest population group in history, baby busters represent the thinnest pool of entry-level workers in modern times. Think about it: during the baby boom years, about 4 million people were born each year; lots of folks to go around and plenty of people to flip the burgers. Contrast that to the period of 1965 to 1980, when only about 3.5 million Americans came kicking and screaming into the harsh light of a delivery room each year.

The pipeline of young workers that traditionally has fueled the American workforce is drying up. According to Census Bureau figures, the number of people age twenty to twenty-nine will shrivel to 34 million by year 2000 (from 41 million in 1980), and they will represent only 13 percent of the population. The Labor Department predicts that the economy will grow by 2 to 3 percent, on average, throughout the nineties. But, the supply of workers will grow by only 1 percent a year. What this means is that a shrinking labor pool, juxtaposed against a huge baby-boomer workforce nearing retirement years, will create a crisis for American business. It's going to be a great deal more difficult to find, attract, hire, motivate, and keep younger workers. There are simply not enough of them to go around.

Johnny and Jane Can't Make Change

Not only will there be fewer young workers than in any decade since 1930, but a shocking percentage of them will lack the skills needed to meet the demands of business and industry. One of the more alarming bits of information about the younger workforce is that, while a higher percentage of them have finished high school, many of them are short on the basic skills needed to perform successfully in today's high-tech world. There is a glaring discrepancy between the education received and the applicable skills that young folks are taking into the workplace. We'll explore this in greater detail in chapter five.

On the surface, the picture looks more positive than it really is. There are actually more college graduates in the workforce today than there are high school dropouts. The quantity of education available is not the problem. The problem is that the pool of available young workers—whether educated or not—is shrinking. Those who dropped out of high school are going to have an increasingly difficult time finding top-paying positions. Because of the shortage of young workers, there will be plenty of opportunities for them to make pizza, wash cars, sell merchandise in a retail store, and perform other low-paying, entry-level jobs. But it is going to be more difficult for the undereducated to make their way through the proverbial jungle out there. They are going to have to clear a career path for themselves with the equivalent of hand shears, while their better-educated counterparts are attacking the corporate jungle with chain saws.

Samuel Halperin, study director for the William T. Grant Foundation, which takes the pulse of the nation's youth, says, "Overall, the tendency in this country has been to assume that when you graduate from high school, you're on your own, you're headed for a life at least as good as your parents' or maybe better. That just isn't true anymore. It's a lot harder for young people to be successful in the world and raise a family."[1]

In chapter five, you'll read in more detail about the skills shortfall facing American business as it recruits younger workers, and how this will affect you, the person who has to train, manage, and motivate them. We'll also offer practical steps you can take to help fill in the gaps for your younger employees, who may lack the basic skills they need.

When Do I Get an Office?

Imagine that you are designing a T-shirt for today's younger worker. What slogan would you emblazon on the front? The question "When do I get an office?" might not be too far off the mark.

Layne A. Longfellow, a psychologist in the behavioral sciences, specializes in helping managers and executives understand the different values of their employees. He has this to say about the generation born and reared in the seventies: "Having grown up taking affluence and continuous economic expansion for granted, it all seems to be coming apart just as they enter the workforce, just as it's their turn to get their piece of the action. They're also terribly cynical and pragmatic. They are not, as they appear, returning to the values of the thirties, forties, and fifties. Theirs is an interest in work that sees work as necessary to support one's real life—a means to an end. The pre-World War II generations, the Depression babies, see work as being real life—an end in itself. The newest generation majors in business and computers because they've concluded that's the best way to get as much as possible as fast as possible; opportunism and pragmatism, not idealism and commitment."[2]

If Longfellow is right, then young workers' attitudes and values about work—getting as much as possible, as fast as possible—are going to clash with the values and attitudes of many of the people who supervise and manage them. Let's take a look at both ends of the young worker spectrum: the high school seniors, who represent the seventeen-year-olds, and the upper ages, the twenty-five-year-olds.

The first chart below summarizes findings from a study done on high school seniors by the Institute for Social Research at the University of Michigan.

What we find most interesting in this information is the marked increase in interest in working for large corporations. If you're a small business owner, you may need to compete with larger corporations for this young talent.

WHERE DO THEY WANT TO WORK?

	Percentage of High School Seniors Who Find These Workplaces Desirable			
	Young Men		*Young Women*	
	1976	*1986*	*1976*	*1986*
Self-employed	51%	50%	35%	41%
A small business	18	18	24	19
A large corporation	15	28	13	26
A social-service organization	8	4	31	21

Source: *Psychology Today,* July 1987, p. 8. Reprinted with permission from *Psychology Today* magazine, copyright © 1987 (Sussex Publishers, Inc.).

WHAT DO THEY WANT FROM THEIR JOBS?

What High School Seniors Rate as Very Important in a Job	*1976*	*1986*
It is interesting to do	88%	87%
Uses skills and abilities	71	72
Predictable, secure future	62	64
Good chance for advancement and promotion	57	67
Chance to make friends	54	53
Chance to earn a good deal of money	47	58
Worthwhile to society	45	41
Chance to participate in decision-making	27	33
High status or prestige	20	32

Source: *Psychology Today,* July 1987, p. 8. Reprinted with permission from *Psychology Today* magazine, copyright © 1987 (Sussex Publishers, Inc.).

What is significant here is that the twentysomething generation is markedly more concerned with advancement, promotion, and earnings than their predecessors.

Careers and Job Security

Looking at these charts, you might conclude that young people entering the workforce are not interested in a career. They are. But having a career does not have the same importance for them as it does for baby boomers. Consider the group now entering corporate America, the twenty-five-year-olds.

Linda Persico signed on at Ford Motor Company in 1987, and was profiled in a *Fortune* cover story that examined the current crop of college-educated twenty-five-year-olds just starting their careers. Linda's father has been an engineer at Ford for thirty years. "I feel guilty for saying this, but I don't feel the kind of loyalty his generation felt. Maybe a career isn't all it's cracked up to be. It's still important to me, but it's not the number one thing in my life."[3]

The baby busters have a strong interest in the quality of life, coupled with interest in a career. But having a career, as Persico states, is not their primary consideration. While many of them realize the importance of moving up in the organization, they would rather ride the corporate elevator than climb the corporate ladder. In contrast to the baby boomers and the World War II-era senior manager and executive, the twentysomething generation is not particularly interested in working its way up to senior leadership from some entry-level position. They want to be valued immediately for the skills they can bring to the workplace.

Job security is not paramount to the baby-buster generation, either. Those who are suitably equipped with marketable job skills know they are living in a seller's market and can move from one job to another, with little or no negative effect. Compare that perception with the one most of us grew up with in the homes of our fathers returning from World War II or the Korean War: Stick it out and make adjustments.

Margaret Regan, a consultant who conducts employee focus groups, says, "The older managers think that if the shoe doesn't fit, you should wear it and walk funny. The baby busters say throw it out and get a new shoe. Their attitude says that they are going to make the choices."[4]

Work is viewed as a means to an end. In contrast to previous generations, this group works to live but does not live to work. Leisure time, flexibility in schedules, and the opportunity to participate in recreational pursuits are high on their agendas. Some of the best and brightest of this new crew are willing to turn down promotions and transfers that might interfere with their lifestyles.

If, at this point, you're scratching your head and wondering what the young workers really want from work, then join the crowd. This is a generation that has not yet identified itself clearly, and it's not one on which a label can easily be pinned. The baby busters, who *Fortune* called "yiffies" for young, individualistic, freedom-minded, and few, seem to be a composite of individuals not cast from any particular mold. They are a jigsaw puzzle; each piece we can fit into place allows us to begin to see the overall portrait a little better.

Attitudes Toward Self and Others

The attitudes baby busters have toward themselves and others provide more clues. A *Time* cover story on the twentysomething generation describes them as having "only a hazy sense of their own identity."[5] That's probably an accurate, if not highly useful, way of viewing young workers. To continue our T-shirt metaphor, if the message on the front is "When Do I Get an Office?," the message on the back may well read, "Second Place Is Okay."

The respondents in the *Time* interviews were unable to clearly define themselves or their generation. They did not identify with any heroes, causes, anthems, or style. On January 16, 1991, a little before 5:00 P.M., the outbreak of war in the Persian Gulf was broadcast on national media. We were having coffee at a cafe near our offices. Our waitress was a pleasant, bright-eyed twenty-year-old. One of us said something to her about the seriousness of the moment. "I hate to seem ignorant," she said, "but do you know what this war is about?"

In childhood, twentysomethings spent more time watching TV than being with their parents. When asked to name a hero, the small number who could come up with one named Ronald Reagan . . . perhaps because of his Hollywood personality?

This generation wishes fervently for the good life, expects less, but hopes it will get at least what its parents got. They want some of whatever is left. One nineteen-year-old, Rebecca Winke, of Madison, Wisconsin, coined the phrase "lurking generation" in describing her peers. "We're waiting in the shadows, quietly figuring out our plan."[6] Whatever that plan might be, it won't be the long-term, work-until-you-drop-or-retire plan of their grandparents, and it won't be the materialistic, BMW-in-the-driveway plan of the yuppies.

A recent *Wall Street Journal,* in describing the new workers, noted they were not locked into career development for the long haul. The gold-watch syndrome is something they both abhor and fear. The *Journal* noted they have "little taste for 'dues paying.' "

One of the common complaints we hear frequently from managers throughout the country is that the young worker wants to start at the top of the mountain, rather than trudge up the corporate trail in the footsteps of those who have gone before. Managers often report the twentysomething crowd seems more interested in listening to a personal radio station with the call letters WII-FM (What's In It For Me?) than in focusing on how they can fit in as team players.

This apparent lack of commitment is maddening, not only to bosses but to parents, teachers, and others who share the young workers' professional and personal lives. There is a sense of cynicism and concern for self first among these young men and women. If they have a commitment, it is to protecting themselves from being hurt. Their risk-taking quotient is low when compared to the entrepreneurial spirit of the baby boomers.

How They See Their World

Try to see the world through the eyes of the baby buster for a minute. You're twenty-four years old and a recent college graduate with a degree in business. You chose a business major because you heard it was the fastest way to get a job and to move up in an organization. But you know you don't want to work yourself to death. You've seen older people in their forties and fifties for whom the job is the end-all and be-all, and you sure don't want to take that route. You want to make enough money to do the things you want to do. But if it means you have to punch the clock day-in and day-out for the next twenty-five years, well, forget it. After all, you're a college graduate and there are lots of jobs where your skills and education can be used. The trick is to find a place that appreciates your unique talents and starts you in a position with responsibility and a good salary right away, then moves you along quickly.

You have a concern for the world and what's happening to it, but you really don't know what you can do about it. As you look at your parents, who grew up in the sixties, you envy them somewhat. They had Vietnam to bind them together; you've heard them talk about the days when they protested the war by occupying the college dean's office. Your dad's best friend was killed in Vietnam. He talks about it as if it were yesterday. The Persian Gulf War was different; most of your generation served willingly. In fact, you feel rather proud of what our young men and women accomplished there. You've seen movies about the sixties and, down deep, you wish there was something going on now that you could feel passionately about. But there's not really a cause these days that grabs and involves you. The problems facing our country are largely the result of those who went before. The way they screwed things up has left a mess for you, and your generation is going to have to live with it.

Thinking about getting married and settling down is important to you, but it is very scary. Your own parents, and those of 40 percent of your peers, are divorced. You remember the loneliness and abandonment you felt when it happened to your family, and you're not going to put your own kids through it. Why take a chance on a lifetime relationship that might not last? Your parents were married by the time they were twenty-four—the age you are now—and were divorced eight years later. You are determined that when *you* get married, it's going to be for keeps. The best way to ensure that is to take your time, maybe live with someone for a while to make sure you want to be together.

You like nice clothes and a car, but you hate the whole "yuppie" thing. You know people in their thirties and forties who have been so driven to get that house in the suburbs, buy a BMW, and wear a Rolex President that they've made work and career the entire focus of their lives. Some of them have been so consumed by their careers that they have never had a relationship with anyone. Hell, some of them have never had an actual date. You definitely are not going to get caught up in that trap. Yes, you are interested in your career and it's important to you, but there are other things in life that are important, like having fun, for instance.

In general, life is pretty okay. You just hope you'll be at least as well off as your own parents, but you aren't optimistic. You hope that you'll get a good job soon and be able to move out of your parents' home.

We hope our little excursion into the consciousness of the baby buster is helpful. Sometimes, stepping into another person's frame of reference is a useful way of getting a handle on how they arrange their mental furniture. If you're a leader of this age group, keep in mind that how they act and what they do is not part of a personal mission to drive you bonkers. They truly see the world through glasses with a unique prescription.

How They Respond to Authority

Many of the managers and executives we've interviewed have voiced another common refrain: young workers today don't respect authority. Katherine Ann Samon, in *Working Woman,* quotes a supervisor, thirty-two, who described an encounter with a young worker, "an entry-level employee, right out of college, who'd been with us three months. At one meeting it turned out we were short one chair. She came in at the same time as a senior manager, saw the one empty chair and grabbed it. Then, when it was our president's turn to speak, this employee rolled her eyes throughout the talk."[7]

Here's a thirty-four-year-old manager's description of her confrontation with a younger worker: "After I was promoted, one of my employees, who is twenty-four, looked me in the eye and said, 'I don't want to report to you. Essentially we're equals doing the same job on the same level. The fact that you're older isn't enough of a reason for you to oversee me.' It was months before I got her to stop submitting her work over my head."[8]

How They View Hierarchy

If you're a thirtysomething or fortysomething manager trying to supervise a twentysomething employee, the examples above probably sound familiar. It's not that the younger worker has no respect for authority, it's just that he or she views the chain of command and the authority-based culture of most organizations as rather odd. In her article, Samon cites Michael Maccoby's explanation of the baby buster's view of organizational hierarchy: "A baby buster working for a traditional manager who believes in hierarchy and position thinks that manager is just funny." Maccoby adds that the primary interest on the part of the baby buster is in whether the person can be important to his or her career, not the title the senior manager holds. Baby busters, he notes, are willing to fit into the hierarchy and take their place, but only if they perceive they'll get something in return.

They Want to Know What's Expected

They operate from a *quid pro quo* perspective in which they constantly expect value received for value given. Maccoby continues, "Busters live in a world of contracts—what do I want from you and what do you expect from me?"[9] The baby busters want to know what is expected of them on the job. They also want to know what they'll get in return if they do what is expected. It goes further than just the duties of the work itself. They want a "you scratch my back and I'll scratch yours" agreement relative to their interpersonal, day-to-day relationships with their supervisors and managers. They have a much greater expectation of being treated as a colleague than the current crop of managers might expect. They want to talk to and associate with upper management, and to actively participate in decision-making. What they don't want is to plod through the traditional chain of command to gain access to senior management. In chapter seven we provide specific steps for making contracts with employees. Experienced managers who have used these techniques report they go a long way toward clarifying expectations and preventing misunderstandings.

They Want to Know Why

A manager in a large insurance corporation told us about one of her younger employees: "She thinks she knows everything, but every time I tell her to do something, the first word out of her mouth is 'Why?' It drives me crazy!"

The new crew wants in on the action. They want to be part of the decision-making process, and they want to know the rationale for the work they are asked to do. This is in marked contrast with the old "organization man" philosophy, which held that when you were told to do something, you did it, no questions asked. When you became a manager, then you could ask the questions. Today's young employee will not work in that kind of environment. "So let 'em find a job somewhere else!" you might say. But remember, the flow of new, qualified workers into the American workplace is getting smaller. By the end of this decade, businesses are going to be scrambling for qualified young people who can do the job. Like it or not, it is the managers who are going to have to do the bulk of the adjusting.

Look at it from an economic point of view. It simply costs a great deal more to seek out, hire, train, benefit, and retain a new employee than it does to keep the ones you now have. So there's going to have to be a new level of patience with the younger worker and his or her insistence upon asking, "Why?"

Are We Having Fun Yet?

One of the most puzzling characteristics about the younger generation is the importance it places on having fun at work. "Fun" has joined the ranks of corporate benefits in its level of importance. Bobby McFerrin's hit song of 1988, "Don't Worry, Be Happy" might be this crowd's anthem, not because they are vacuous, but because it's part of their psychological makeup.

Keep in mind that this is a generation reared by a surrogate parent—television. These are the latchkey children you've read about who came home from school to their nicely furnished but parentally absent homes, waiting for the sound of the BMW and the Volvo their parents drove from respective jobs. They did not live the life portrayed on "Leave It To Beaver," where June sent Wally and Beaver off in the morning and was there to greet them in the afternoon when they came home from school. Today's young workers had to entertain themselves in their childhood years, so the pursuit of entertainment became the major component in the time they spent alone while their parents worked.

The notion that work should be fun is disturbing to many mainline managers. Most of us in our thirties and forties were reared in homes in which our World War II-veteran fathers dutifully trudged off to work each day to do jobs they may or may not have liked. The concept of "fun" at work was only a coincidental occurrence. Not so for the twentysomething crowd. They have been nursed by a national media that is among the best in the world. They've never truly been weaned from that electronic surrogate which fed them a diet of "fun" throughout their growing-up years.

Now you've been introduced to the twentysomething generation. They are an enigma, to be sure. They are aggressive, ambitious, extroverted, self-oriented, conservative, and career-focused. They are not worried about job security. They are largely uninterested in current affairs, afraid of failing at marriage, inquisitive, individualistic, and demand their piece of whatever action is left.

We've painted a fairly bleak picture. It's important to remember, though, that no matter how we're raised, we still have a choice. And many of the twentysomethings have made outstanding choices. There are many who are extraordinary. Not every twentysomething has all the characteristics we've described. Our research indicates, though, that a significant number of young workers seventeen to twenty-seven exhibit the traits we've profiled here and elsewhere in the book.

In the chapters to follow, you'll increase your understanding of what makes workers between the ages of seventeen and twenty-seven tick. You'll also learn more about how they got to be the way they are, the value systems that drive them, how the workforce will change from its present monochrome hue to a brightly colored rainbow of ethnic groups, the skills shortfall and what to do about it, day-to-day leadership techniques that work, what turns them on, and what turns them off.

In our Introduction, we promised to provide you with practical applications and techniques that can be used immediately to better supervise and manage the young worker. At the end of each chapter you'll find an application called "Taking Action," designed to help you get the most from the material in a particular chapter. Some readers may like to take pen in hand and complete these assessments, questionnaires, and worksheets.

TAKING ACTION

While this chapter has introduced the twentysomething generation in a broad sense, it may be useful for you to focus for a few minutes on one or two of the young employees you manage or supervise. The questionnaire below will help you to increase your understanding of this individual. Maybe you should choose an employee with whom you are currently having a problem.

Employee Questionnaire

The employee's name:

_____

His or her educational background:

_____

What he/she does for fun outside of work:

_____

This person's greatest talent:

_____

What he/she expects from me:

_____

What this person does that drives me crazy (focus on *behavior*):

_____

What I wish he/she would do instead:

_____

What I need to do to help him/her:

_____

Notes

1. "Transition to Adulthood Harder for '80's Youth," *Denver Post,* August 25, 1988, p. 6.

CHAPTER-AT-A-GLANCE

- Born between 1965 and 1972, the baby busters represent a decided drop in the birth curve when compared to all previous years.

- They represent the thinnest pool of entry-level workers in modern times.

- Even though a higher number of them have finished high school, many are short the basic skills needed to perform successfully in today's high-tech world.

- There are more college graduates in the workforce today than there are high school dropouts.

- The twentysomething generation is markedly more concerned with advancement, promotion, and earnings than their predecessors.

- They have a strong interest in the quality of life coupled with interest in a career, but a career is not their primary consideration.

- Young workers are not particularly interested in working their way up to senior management from the entry level. They want to be valued immediately for the skills they bring to the workplace.

- Baby busters view the chain of command and authority-based culture in organizations as odd. What matters is whether or not the person above them is important to their careers. They are willing to fit into the hierarchy only if they perceive they will get something in return.

- They want to talk to and associate with upper management and to actively participate in decision-making without having to plod through the traditional chain of command.

- Raised by their surrogate parent, television, they carry the notion that work should be fun.

- The twentysomethings do not rally to political or social causes, and they rarely have heroes or heroines.

2. Layne A. Longfellow, "Ethics to Excellence: You Just Can't Get Good Help Anymore," Presentation at Clearwater Beach, Florida, April 2, 1989.
3. Alan Deutschman, "What 25-Year-Olds Want," *Fortune,* August 27, 1990, p. 43.
4. Ibid.
5. David M. Gross and Sophronia Scott, "Proceeding With Caution," *Time,* July 16, 1990, p. 57.
6. Ibid.
7. Katherine Ann Samon, "The Brash Pack," *Working Woman,* August 1990, p. 68.
8. Ibid.
9. Ibid.

2

When Manager and Worker Don't See Eye-to-Eye

We hear all sorts of horror stories from managers about their younger workers. In this chapter, we share one of them with you. You'll have an opportunity to experience the feelings and frustrations of a seasoned manager. If you are supervising young workers, we believe her story will sound familiar to you.

The chapter is patterned after "Can This Marriage Be Saved?," the most popular women's magazine feature in the world, appearing in *Ladies' Home Journal* for thirty-six years. The case in this chapter is based on interviews and information from our files. The story is true; the names and details have been changed to maintain confidentiality.

You'll hear the manager's story first. Her comments will acquaint you with the complaints we hear most often about the twentysomething generation. Then you'll have a chance to view the situation from another perspective—the younger worker's. Finally, we'll tell you how we, as consultants, handled this case: the prognosis and our recommendations. We think this last section will offer you some practical ideas on how to work more effectively with your younger employees.

The Manager's Turn

"I was floored. It was Mike's first-year performance review—a year of less than mediocre work from him—and he expected a promotion!" said forty-year-old Dolores in frustration, as she pulled off her glasses and leaned back in her swivel desk chair.

"This is not the way I was in my first year on the job. I truly cared about the quality of work I produced, and I would have done anything to get my boss's approval. Mike seems to think the world ought to be handed to him on a silver platter. I arrived at work knowing I would have to pay my dues.

"He's my copywriter, but his writing skills are almost nonexistent. What's happened to the education system in this country? I graduated from high school knowing the difference between a noun and a verb. Mike doesn't seem to know or care.

"Just last week he handed in his assignment for the marketing brochure for our new product. Not only was his manuscript three days late, but it was poorly written, full of misspelled words and grammatical errors, and some of the technical information was just plain wrong.

"Okay, I should have given him better guidance on the project. Maybe I should have set up some interim meetings with him. Some of the other supervisors just seem to have a knack with their younger staff, and I can't compete with that. Still, I don't have the time to hold Mike's hand every step of the way.

"I have the impression that, as far as Mike is concerned, I don't do anything right. Yesterday I overheard him complaining about me to some of his friends in the coffee room. I know I blew up at him over his brochure copy. What can I say? I have high expectations—for myself and for everyone who works for me.

"I'm sure he'll also tell you I keep him in the dark about what's going on here in the company. Well, what does he expect? When he becomes a loyal, motivated employee, I'll be glad to include him in meetings and involve him in decisions.

"His biggest problem is his own self-interest. The other people on my staff are team players. Mike isn't. He only seems to care about what's in it for him.

"This company means a lot to me. When I hired Mike, I thought he felt the same way, but clearly I was wrong. His latest request to go on flextime, so he can have more daylight hours to ride his motorcycle, shows just how much this job means to him.

"When we're working on a tight deadline and everybody pulls together to put in the hours it takes to complete a project, where's Mike? Out the door the minute the clock strikes five o'clock.

"This job is my life. I grew up in the sixties. My first job was in a neighborhood food co-op where everybody cared deeply about the work we were doing. We weren't paid a lot, but we did everything meticulously—and we worked together. There was a sense of harmony; I can't think of any other way of saying it.

"I feel like I've been able to create a pretty similar feeling here in this department. There is a real sense of sharing among my staff. We know and care about each other as people, and we know we can count on each other. There's a dependability and a loyalty here that I wouldn't trade for anything.

"I never thought I'd be talking to a management consultant about how to handle somebody on my staff. I'm a good leader, and I know how to motivate people to do a good job. But Mike is different. The way I normally work with people doesn't cut it with Mike.

"I'm frustrated and resentful about the position he's got me in here, and I have to admit he causes me to question my communication skills and management techniques.

"To tell you the truth, I'm not even sure I'm even willing to do anything differently when it comes to managing Mike. He's the one who needs to change."

Mike's Turn

"Dolores may think the brochure I wrote last week was no good, but I worked damn hard on it. I just have no idea how to please her," said Mike, a bright-faced twenty-two-year-old. "She was way too busy to tell me what she wanted, so I had to do the best I could with very little information.

"Look, I know I'm not Dolores's idea of the perfect employee. She's totally devoted to this place, and, frankly, for me it's just a job. The things that really matter to me don't happen within the concrete walls of this place.

"Dolores reminds me a lot of my own parents. They're into their careers just the way she is—and they're all workaholics. I've had a good firsthand look at that lifestyle. It's not for me.

"My folks never had time for me. They were always off to another meeting or staying late to finish a project. I won't have a family until I'm sure I'll be able to devote the quality time to my kids that I never got from my parents.

"Work isn't the only thing in life, and I'd tell Dolores that if I didn't think she'd fire me for it. I ride motocross races on the weekends. That's what really matters to me. I like the people, and I like the fun.

"Fun is the element that's really missing here for me on this job. Everybody seems so darn serious about everything.

"In all honesty, I expected a lot more from a job. I've got a business degree, and I thought it would get me more than it has. To tell you the truth, I'm just a glorified file clerk and proofreader. The work is tedious and boring.

"My senior year in college, I worked for a semester as a press aide in the governor's office. It was great. I had an office of my own, and they treated me like I was real important. I guess maybe in some ways that was actually a negative experience for me, because I came to work here expecting a lot more respect and responsibility.

"I guess I want to please Dolores, but she's a very difficult boss. I was totally surprised to sit down with her for my first-year review and hear about all her complaints. I mean, I knew she didn't like this last brochure, but, other than that, she has never said anything about my work.

"All this time, I thought I was doing okay. I wish she would just tell me when I mess up. It's the only way I'm going to learn.

"Despite what she tells everybody, she's not the most open person in the world. Whenever I come up with a creative suggestion, she treats me like a high school kid who's not old enough to know what he's talking about.

"Dolores is living in a dream world. I'm sick of hearing about the sixties, Martin Luther King, JFK, and all the rest. When we went to war in the Persian Gulf, I don't know why we didn't just wipe out Saddam Hussein and be done with it. What's to protest? There were some good ideas in the sixties, but it just didn't work. I'm going to take care of myself. I want a job that pays well, that's fun, that doesn't interfere with my outside life. If this one doesn't get better real soon, I'm out of here."

Our Turn

The first year on the job is as critical to an employee's development as the first year of a baby's life. The manager has a tremendous responsibility to "parent" the new employee well. Mike is projecting many of his issues with his parents onto Dolores; to manage him well requires dealing with those issues.

Mike is typical in many ways of today's new crop of employees: self-interested, unwilling to "pay dues," poorly educated, impatient, and skeptical.

Yet, replacing Mike at this point may not be a wise move. The shrinking labor pool will not guarantee a more outstanding replacement. Also, Dolores has invested too much energy to let Mike go without trying a few simple strategies to improve his work performance.

Our first step was to help Dolores understand that Mike *did* care about his job and *was* motivated. Mike's values and beliefs—about careers, about work environments, about bosses—are completely different from Dolores's. As long as she expects him to change so that he views the work world the same way she does, she will fail to manage and motivate him successfully.

There is important work to be done when a new young worker is hired. To be effective, the manager must outline very specific concrete responsibilities, goals, performance standards, communication paths, opportunities for personal advancement, and rewards. Dolores made the mistake many experienced managers make: she assumed that Mike is basically the same as she is, that he is motivated by the same things she is, and that his work standards match hers. This is a dangerous assumption, since Mike sees the world through a totally different frame of reference. Since Mike is unaware of Dolores's expectations, he has an unrealistic view about prospects of getting promoted at the end of his first year. Mike needs to know the exact amount of dues to pay. He needs specific standards to measure up to.

We used Mike's first-year anniversary with the company as an opportunity to work with Dolores and Mike to spell these things out. We actually developed a written contract with specific follow-up dates that would govern Mike's next six months with the company. The contract helps Mike to see exactly what it will take for him to perform adequately with this company. (You'll read more about developing contracts with young employees and see a sample of an actual contract in chapter seven.)

Mike was not getting the constant feedback from Dolores that he needed. He was unaware, until just the week before his first-year performance appraisal, that his work was unsatisfactory. Dolores was uncomfortable giving feedback, especially when it was negative. So she gave Mike hints that she assumed he understood. We worked with her to find new ways to discipline Mike, giving him specific information about his behavior—not his personality—at the time the behavior occurred. Dolores soon found she was more comfortable expressing her criticism. She grew less likely to allow her anger to build up to explosive proportions, decreasing the likelihood of ugly confrontations like the one over the poorly written brochure.

Like so many workers from the baby bust generation, Mike's basic skills were poor. Yet, he was unaware that his writing was not acceptable. Dolores discussed this problem with him and was surprised how easy it was to convince him he needs to improve his writing skills. He saw clearly that those skills are critical to his future success on the job market. Dolores found a good basic-writing-skills program at a local community college, and Mike enrolled for one evening a week.

Mike wanted to spend more time with Dolores, which caught her unawares. But an overwhelming majority of today's kids feel their parents didn't spend enough time with them. A recent *Time* article on the twentysomething generation reports that 64 percent say they will spend more time with their own kids than their parents spent with them.[1] Dolores now sees that by becoming Mike's boss she stepped into a parenting role for him—whether she wanted that role or not. We suggested she let Mike in on the action by including him in meetings and decision-making. She reluctantly agreed to this, and has spent more one-on-one time with Mike. They are developing a personal relationship—much like a coach and player—that we believe will make a significant difference in Mike's performance.

Mike's need for fun on the job was not being met. Certainly all of us want to have fun, but we find this to be a critical factor to job satisfaction for the twentysomething generation. Dolores developed a more light-hearted approach with Mike, and together they developed some "games" related to work goals—with payoffs for achievement. For example, when Mike completes a goal, Dolores gives him a brief "attaboy" on a yellow Post-it note. After he collects ten of these, Dolores arranges flextime so he can leave a few minutes early Friday afternoon for his motocross racing.

It is easy to forget that most of the work we give our entry-level employees is humdrum and often tedious. Supervisors at Disneyland and Disney World use games to motivate workers. They get candy bars and extra time for breaks when, for example, they "find the guest who has traveled the most miles to get to the park."

"I try to make something different every day," says one Disney leader. "My employees answer the same questions and perform the same job day after day. We have to provide some magic for them."[2]

For Mike, these games now add a bit of levity; he has something to look forward to on even the most routine of days.

Finally, it was important for Dolores to hear that work is truly not the number one priority for Mike and many of his counterparts. In fact, outside interests and relationships often rank higher. Dolores loves her job and is deeply committed to her work, but to expect that same love and commitment from Mike is unrealistic. When she understood the importance of hobbies in Mike's life, she was able to shift her expectations. Mike wanted a flextime schedule; this actually worked out well for everyone because Mike now staffs the office during early morning hours when no one else wants to work.

Perhaps it sounds as if the burden for change fell on Dolores, when it may appear to you the culprit was actually Mike. However, Dolores *did* need to adapt her leadership style to be more effective with Mike. As a leader you may need to do the same. You are the older, more mature person. Your young workers are still developing their ability to negotiate and take responsibility for their behaviors. They need your help. We reassured Dolores that she was doing a great job with most of the people in her department. At the same time, she was using leadership skills developed for workers her own age and older.

Certainly Mike has many changes to make if he is going to keep his job. His basic skills must improve. He must become a better team player. He must become more self-reliant. In short, he will have to pay his dues. We helped Dolores to be a more effective coach, so that Mike could grow more efficiently and less painfully into the employee Dolores needs.

The reality is that most work situations include people with divergent views on ethics, standards, goals, processes, and nearly every issue that comes along. In short, you will almost never be working with a staff of people who are just like you. Sometimes our differences get in the way of productive work relationships; the better we understand and appreciate our unique differences, the more likely we are to produce an effective, efficient work environment. In chapter three, we'll examine the new worker's unique set of values and delve into the question: how did they get this way?

TAKING ACTION

Here are five suggestions you can use right now to more successfully lead and motivate the typical twentysomething employee:

- Consider yourself a "parent" in the employee's first months.
- Get together with him/her to outline *specific* responsibilities, goals, performance standards, communication paths, opportunities for personal advancement, and rewards. (Yes, you should have done this when the person was first hired, but it's never too late to get started.)
- Be willing to lay it on the line when undesirable behaviors crop up. Remember, young employees are hungry for feedback. Explore helpful ways of delivering criticism.
- Spend time with your young workers.
- Encourage them to find creative ways to have fun while getting the job done.

Notes

1. *Time,* "Proceeding with Caution," July 16, 1990, p. 62.
2. Charlene Marmer Solomon, "How Does Disney Do It?," *Personnel Journal,* December 1989, pp. 56, 57.

CHAPTER-AT-A-GLANCE

• Manager's perspective on young workers:

Dominated by self-interest.
Lacking motivation.
Noncaring attitude.
Think the world should be handed to them on a silver platter.
Lack of loyalty.

• Young worker's perspective:

It's just a job; being a workaholic is not the lifestyle for me.
Fun is missing from the job.
A job shouldn't interfere with outside life.

• Consultant's perspective:

To be effective, managers must outline specific, concrete responsibilities, goals and performance standards, communication paths and opportunities for advancement, and rewards for the young worker.
Do not assume that your young workers have the same values and views of work as you do, or that they are motivated by the same things you are.
Discipline yourself to focus on the behavior, not the personality, at the time undesirable behavior occurs.
Because many young workers were latchkey kids, they crave time with their managers, time they were deprived of with their parents.
Most work we give to entry-level workers is tedious and humdrum; it's not much fun.
The number one priority for the majority of young workers is not work, but outside interests and relationships.

Kids! I don't know what's wrong with these kids today. . . .
Why can't they be like we were, perfect in every way?
What's the matter with kids today?
—From *Bye-Bye Birdie,*
lyrics by Lee Adams and Charles Strouse

What have you done for me lately?
—Worker, age twenty-three

3

Does Anything Matter to Them?

It's true: kids just aren't the same as they used to be. We see major changes in this twentysomething generation, and many of these changes have to do with values. Chapter three is critical to an understanding of younger workers because it gives you an overview of their beliefs, attitudes, goals and expectations. It will also tell you why they hold these values—what shaped them, culturally and historically. We offer you the why because we find managers and supervisors are frustrated about new worker values, and people usually deal better with their frustrations when they understand the causes.

In this chapter, we introduce you to a values model called the MindMaker6™, which gives you a useful, practical tool for better understanding and dealing with values differences. We tell you what one smart business school is doing to deal with the values gap. Finally, we give you three new tools you can use today that will make you a values-savvy leader.

Twentysomething Values

All humans have beliefs, constraints, boundaries, and conditions that they take for granted. These values make up the essence of our personal philosophy and govern the way we operate in our lives. Although every individual has a unique, personal set of values, generations historically develop widespread, pervasive belief systems.

A tremendously valuable resource for understanding the baby busters' values is a yearly report by the Higher Education Research Institute based at UCLA. *The American Freshman: Twenty Year Trends* has tracked the values of nearly 300,000 college freshman per year for two decades. The report verifies dramatic differences between the college freshman of the sixties and the eighties, and it is one of the sources we have used in determining the values of the twentysomething generation.

Our research points to a set of eight core values. Certainly not every member of the generation holds exactly these values. Just as certainly, each of these eight values has profoundly affected the lives of nearly every twentysomething worker.

1. They are self-oriented.
Perhaps the most obvious value of today's men and women seventeen to twenty-seven is a strong self-orientation. Their first priority is themselves. In *The American Freshman,* the personal values showing the greatest decline in recent years are those having to do with helping others.[1] There has been a strong decline in altruistic careers such as nursing, social work, and teaching.[2] Although these young people tend to be social creatures, they want to know, "What's in it for me?" before making decisions or taking action.

2. They feel cynical.
Twentysomething workers don't feel the idealism of the sixties generation. Here's an amazing thought: not one of these folks is old

enough to remember John F. Kennedy's assassination. For previous American generations, November 22, 1963, holds tremendous meaning. Today's young people don't have even a memory of the idealistic young president whom the sixties generation revered, and they don't have the sixties causes, either. They sense that sixties kids felt they made a difference, that they were part of something important. That idealism offered a stabilizing influence.

This generation yearns for a cause, yet they are cynical about the activism and idealism of the sixties. They believe they inherited a polluted earth, a racially fractured society, overwhelming social problems, and the constant threat of nuclear annihilation. They see the chaos in the Soviet Union, the massacre of young Chinese in Tiananmen Square, the occupation of Kuwait, and the subsequent Persian Gulf War as further evidence of a world gone mad. They tend to have a gloomy outlook, feeling paralyzed by the problems confronting the United States. A recent study of 1,000 young people conducted by Peter Hart Research Associates found that nearly half are worried that the United States' best years are past. A recent special edition of *Newsweek* reports that 45 percent of our teens feel the world is getting worse. Sixty-two percent feel their lives will be harder than their parents'.[3] In the UCLA survey, the category "developing a meaningful philosophy of life," most popular in 1967 (83 percent), continued to plummet to less than 40 percent.[4]

We recently heard a story from a young friend, Kevin Riddle. It's something he found particularly compelling. As the story goes, an African villager, with a herd of beautiful black-and-white cows, found suddenly one morning that they had stopped producing milk. Since he had recently moved them to a new pasture, he returned them to the pasture where they had grazed before. Alas, the next morning, there was still no milk. So the farmer decided to watch the cows all night to see if he could find the problem. In the middle of the night, he was astounded to see a flock of beautiful celestial women descending on silken silver cords. Each filled a gourd with milk.

When the farmer tried to catch them, they quickly scattered. But he was able to catch one, the loveliest, who agreed to become the farmer's wife. Together they went to his home. She brought along her basket, which she explained contained her magic, and she warned him never to look inside. The farmer and his beautiful celestial wife lived happily for many years. But, as one might guess, one day while the wife worked in the fields, her husband's curiosity got the better of him and he looked inside the basket. At first, he just stared in disbelief. Then he burst into laughter. When she returned, she knew immediately what had happened.

"You have broken your word," she said. "You looked in the basket."

"Silly woman," he said, "there was nothing in there."

At that, she turned and walked into the sunset, never to be seen again. She went away—not so much because he had broken his word—but because he was blind to the magic contained in the basket. The farmer lived the rest of his life in loneliness. "The story," this younger worker told me, "is an accurate metaphor for my generation. We seem to have lost the magic, or perhaps we're just not able to see it." It's no wonder some social scientists have dubbed this group the "why bother? generation."

3. They are materialistic.

The young worker wants money, power, and status. A recent poll conducted by marketing professor Kenneth Bernhardt of Georgia State University shows young people want to spend their money on stereos, clothes, cars, and dating.[5] A recent news story profiled today's college-dormitory residents. Colleges and universities around the country are having to rewire their dormitories to accommodate the increased power demands of students' stereos, VCR's, CD players, cappuccino makers, and computers. Gone are the days when a college student's dorm room had only an alarm clock and record player.

Being well-off financially is *the* item in the UCLA survey showing the most dramatic increase. It is rated higher today than at any time in the twenty-two years the annual sample has been taken.[6] A record 75 percent listed "being well off financially" as their first priority.[7] The Adolph Coors Company recently polled 1,044 students twenty-one years or older about their top priority when considering a job. Salary was number one, with 74 percent expecting to make up to $50,000 a year in their first job.[8] In colleges across the nation, occupation-oriented majors are the hottest draw on campus, presumably because they offer the best possibility for high-paying jobs; the business major has gained steadily for two decades and is the number one choice of college students today.

Twentysomething workers even view themselves in financial terms. They see themselves as marketable commodities. They constantly look for ways to upgrade their value on the market that needs them so badly. "They are keenly aware of their own marketability," says Katherine Tanelian, worldwide communication personnel manager for Hewlett-Packard in Palo Alto, California.[9] They know they are desperately needed on the job market; every restaurant and store they pass has a "help wanted" sign in the window. Have you tried to get a babysitter or a kid to mow your grass lately?

4. Their adolescence is extended.
For those just getting started, the American Dream is now incredibly difficult to achieve. They know it, and they are postponing moving into adult roles as long as possible. "A whole lot of indicators tell us that adolescence now extends into the early twenties," says labor economist Martha Farnsworth.[10] They are waiting longer to marry. The average marriage age (twenty-six for men; twenty-four for women) is the highest of the century.[11] They are postponing careers, taking longer to get through college, and living with their parents. In January 1990, the Census Bureau reported that 22 million young adults over age eighteen are living at home, almost a 50 percent increase since 1970.[12]

5. They want quantity time.

We remember from our own childhoods that the last thing we wanted was more time with our parents. As a matter of fact, we were delighted by an evening with a babysitter or a week at summer camp because it gave us a break. Not so with today's kids, who feel they've been rushed through life. They believe they were deprived of time: to be kids, to play and grow, and, most important, to be with their parents. Our friends' children tell us their ideal day is a day spent with Mom or Dad—or better yet, both. The twentysomething generation is absolutely committed to spending more time with their own children. Psychologists often say we're motivated by what we didn't get as children, and for this generation that's *time*.

6. They want to have fun.

Managers across the nation complain the new generation has a terrible work ethic. They report that *fun* seems to be the young workers' first priority. Our research verifies that this generation views work in a completely different way.

Quality of life is more important to them than the job—they see their jobs as vehicles to get them what they want. They are only mildly interested in careers. Strong outside interests take precedence over work. They relish leisure time and are committed to a high quality of life. Katherine Tanelian of Hewlett-Packard says, "They ask almost as many questions about the work environment as the jobs they'll be doing and the pay."[13] Alexander Astin, director of the UCLA survey, says, "The idea for them is that work and schooling is something you do to get to something else, rather than something you do which should be fulfilling in and of itself."[14]

7. They are slow to commit.

Baby busters are not as loyal to companies and employers as are older generations. When they do make a commitment, it is one they've taken plenty of time to evaluate. This lack of willingness to commit is reflected in their dating and mating habits. Ask any high school student: young people today tend to hang out in groups rather than to make a commitment to just one boyfriend or girlfriend.

8. They don't bow to authority.
Younger workers will not respect you just because you're the boss. They want to know *why* they're being asked to do things. They question authority, and they have a disregard for hierarchies. They take for granted that they will be involved in decisions. Data from the "1988 Freshman Survey" point to strong support for student activism—being involved in faculty retention decisions and having a role in the actual running of their schools.[15] By the way, the study does not confirm the popular belief that young people today are politically conservative. True, when they compare their politics to those of the vocal sixties group, they label themselves "middle of the road." However, the research shows they agree with most positions commonly linked with liberalism.

To put this all together, then, here are the eight key values of the twentysomething generation:

- They are self-oriented.
- They feel cynical.
- They are materialistic.
- Their adolescence is extended.
- They want quantity time.
- They want to have fun.
- They are slow to commit.
- They don't bow to authority.

Here's how we see this set of twentysomething values in contrast to the values of two previous generations:

	World War II Generation	Baby-Boom Generation	Twentysomething Generation
Birth Years	1925–1945	1946–1964	1965–1975
personal	allegiance	self-discovery	self-oriented
political	conservative	liberal	pseudo-conservative
social	law and order	altruistic, humanistic	competitive
ethical	fundamental	moralistic	situational
financial	save and pay cash	buy now/pay later	almost hopeless
buying	based on necessity	have it now	whoever has the most wins
products	home appliances, tools, homes, cars	clothes, entertainment, travel	high-tech gadgets for work and fun
reward	"I earned it."	"You owe me."	"I want it, but may not be able to get it."

Desert Storm: From the MTV Generation to the CNN Generation

Whether the Persian Gulf War had a significant impact on the twentysomething generation's values will not be known for a few years. Certainly, young people in the United States made the country proud. Forced to "answer the wake-up call of world events," they responded with courage, loyalty, and precision.[16] No longer were they just the small group of people younger than the baby boom; they were suddenly a pivotal part of the country's history. According to a *USA Today* survey of 729 twentysomethings, nearly two-thirds supported the U.S. war policy.[17]

Certainly the war caused the twentysomething generation to examine their values and beliefs. Says Alan Fisher, of Garland, Texas, "We are rarely exposed to ideals which suggest trying for the sake of the experience, helping without expecting reward, or achieving success without displaying arrogance."

"Once the baby boomers are dead and gone," states James McColly of Idaho, "and my generation is done cleaning up their mess and paying all their bills, we will start caring and thinking about somebody other than just ourselves."[18]

How Did They Get This Way?

The experts tell us we get our values from the culture and world events with which we grow up. Morris Massey, an expert in values clarification, says our values are programmed in by about age six. Layne Longfellow, who speaks on generational values, explains it this way: "The way I see the world is the result of the world I've seen."

So, to understand the "why bother?" generation, it is helpful to look at the world surrounding them from birth to age six. Basically, that was 1970s America, the Watergate decade. It was the post-baby-boom decade. By the way, it would be easy to blame ourselves for twentysomething values. As the parents and teachers of this generation, we are at least partially responsible for the way they turned out. However, we can't change the past; we can only deal with what we find in front of us now. So we recommend avoiding the blame issue and knuckling down to learn as much as possible about what makes this twentysomething generation tick.

Five Influences That Most Shaped Today's Young Workers

1. Parenting
Families are fundamentally different today. Even the way we define "family" has changed. In 1960, a "family" consisted of: one wage-

earning dad, one housekeeping mom, and one or more children. Seventy percent of the families in the United States met those criteria. Today only 15 percent fit the leave-it-to-Beaver profile.[19]

In many ways, the kids of the twentysomething generation raised themselves. According to Paul Hirsch, a Chicago sociologist, "This generation came from a culture that really didn't prize having kids, anyway. Their parents just wanted to go and play out their roles. They assumed the kids were going to grow up all right." About 40 percent of them were children of divorce. Even more were latchkey kids; their parents were still in the middle of their workday when these kids got home from school in the afternoon.[20] A popular radio and television message to parents in the sixties was, "It's ten o'clock. Do you know where your children are?" The latchkey child might be asked, "It's six o'clock. Do you know where your parents are?"

This generation grew up with parents who, by and large, defined themselves according to their jobs and where a significant number of parents might be called workaholics. Their kids resented these absentee parents and decided to live their lives differently. They don't want their jobs to equal their identities, and they're unwilling to become workaholics. For most of them, second place is just fine.

2. Declining numbers

Demographically, this generation simply doesn't have the numbers the sixties generation had. Today, the baby boomers account for one-third of the population of the United States. The birth rate when the twentysomethings were born was half of what it was during the early years of the baby boom. For the next two decades, the boomers will be in their prime, at their peak earning power. In contrast, today's young people feel irrelevant.

The following chart helps explains this. In the sixties and seventies, the United States was dominated by its young people, the 76 million post–World War II babies. There were simply more of them than anyone else. Today, there are about equal numbers of people of all ages.

PERCENTAGE OF AMERICAN POPULATION BY AGE

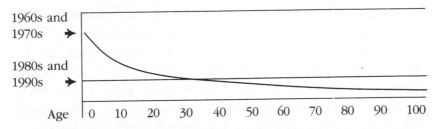

3. Economic turbulence

When we ask people in our seminars about the seventies, we find the most typical response is a blank stare. Not much was memorable about that decade, the one that shaped the values of our young workers. The two things people tend to remember are Watergate and dramatic economic upheaval. Today's young workers saw their country's leaders discredited, and they came of age during the high inflation of the late seventies and the dramatic recession of the early eighties.

This economic turbulence had a profound impact on them. A recent *Seventeen* magazine survey found that 75 percent of today's teenagers are worried they won't have enough money when they get older. Bob McBride, an Adolph Coors director, notes that in Coors' survey of college students twenty-one and older, salary moved into top priority this year, whereas in last year's survey, students rated advancement and responsibility more important. "Given today's economic outlook," says McBride, "students may feel that salary is now a more important consideration."[21] The American Council on Education survey "reflects a rising tide of materialism coupled with student concern about an uncertain economic future."[22] They fear they will never have the financial stability to own their own homes, provide their families with a high quality of life, or put their children through college. These fears are certainly worthy of more than passing thought in light of current costs for homes, cars, and college educations, especially in proportion to today's declining salaries.

4. Instant knowledge

The media and the entertainment industry have dramatically influenced this generation—more than any generation before them. In homes where the parents were absent, the television became the foster parent. That foster parent had a grim message. In 1991, the Persian Gulf War became the ultimate video game for the video generation.[23] Layne A. Longfellow points out that, for other generations, regular doses of electronic bad news have been only a recent addition to our lives. But the twentysomething generation has been surrounded by daily doses of doom and gloom from birth. By age sixteen, the average young person has seen 33,000 murders on TV and in the movies.[24]

In the seventies, Watergate unfolded before their very eyes, right alongside "The Jeffersons" and "Let's Make a Deal." Watergate left them skeptical about leadership in general. A recent *Time*/CNN survey asked them about heroes. They failed to agree on any; the top-ranked hero (Reagan) received only 8 percent of the vote.[25]

5. Stress

Never has growing up in America been so stressful. Marc Miringoff of Fordham University tabulates the *Index of Social Health for Children and Youth*. In 1987—the latest year for which statistics are available—the index was at its lowest point in twenty years.[26] So 1987 was the most stressful year since 1967. As 1991 began, the key players in the Persian Gulf War were thousands of men and women age seventeen to twenty-seven. Those who didn't go to the Middle East worried about their friends in combat, about the possible reactivation of the draft. In some parts of the urban United States, young African-American men worried about surviving street combat.

A Generational Values Model

To better understand younger workers, we've found it helpful to step back and take a look at values systems from a larger perspective. A helpful tool is the MindMaker6™, published by Brain Technologies Corporation. The MindMaker6™ is based on the work of industrial psychologist Clare Graves and incorporates seventeen years of research by Ken Adams at Hewlett-Packard.

The MindMaker6™ presents a model for understanding six sets of values. The first two values systems, Kinsperson and Loner, originally developed thousands of years ago when people were nomadic, living off the land and struggling to survive.

Kinsperson

This values system developed when people began to band together in order to survive. Kinspeople value survival, cooperation, and ancestry. They feel a sense of magic about the earth and its wonders. Although Kinsperson is an ancient system, it continues to offer richness and meaning to those who subscribe to it. American workers who hold this values system have the survival of their family or group at heart.[27]

With the growing number of immigrants and ethnic minorities in the new labor pool, you may be supervising more young workers with Kinsperson values than before. When you hire young workers who have been influenced by gangs during their adolescence, you may find they display strong Kinsperson values.

Loner

While Kinspeople gathered together to survive, the Loner struggled independently. The Loner system honors strength and survival of the fittest. Loners believe in a concrete, black-and-white, dog-eat-dog world where the toughest make it. There is a relatively small number of American workers who hold these beliefs. But abused children can become Loners as adults, and the number of abused children is skyrocketing. Sooner or later you may find yourself supervising a Loner.

Loyalist and Achiever, the next two systems, developed along with industrialization and capitalism. Together, they explain the beliefs that traditionally have been used to describe what it means to be American.

Loyalist

The Loyalist system historically united large groups of diverse people with a body of rules and regulations. Loyalists cherish law and order. They support the traditional business pyramid with one honored leader at the helm. "Group oriented and conservative, Loyalists value duty, honor, respect, and authority."[28] Certainly, no Americans are untouched by Loyalist values, and the majority hold this as their primary system. The reemergence of fraternities and sororities on many college campuses leads us to believe we will continue to see large numbers of Loyalists in the ranks of the younger worker.

Achiever

Achiever values developed along with Loyalist values. While the Loyalist system united groups of people, the Achiever is a self-oriented values system that capitalizes on trade and commerce. Achievers value competition, winning, status, and reward. They enjoy work environments that allow them to succeed at reaching goals.

The twentysomething worker's orientation toward self and materialism reflect Achiever values, and a deeper understanding of how to manage and motivate Achievers is invaluable to supervisors struggling with younger employees.

The last two systems, Involver and Choice-Seeker, are relatively recent. This doesn't mean folks didn't have these values before; the beginning of the information age found much larger groups of people holding these values:

Involver

This is the values system the baby-boom generation is best known for and which clashed with Loyalist and Achiever values in the sixties. To understand Involver values, check out a videotape of the movie *The Big Chill,* or catch an episode of "thirtysomething" on television. The Involver cherishes cooperation and a sense of community. Involvers are skeptical of authority and expect to be included in decisions that affect them. They believe in equality, activism, and harmony.

If you are a supervisor or manager born between 1946 and 1964, chances are you were strongly influenced by these values. Though many young workers have rejected these values, we find significant numbers who share them.

Choice-Seeker

Born in the information age, the Choice-Seeker system is based on "what works." Choice-Seekers are highly individualistic people who often have technical expertise. They are interested in systems and how they operate. Choice-Seekers cherish privacy, information, and competence. They place little importance on how they are seen by others.

The Choice-Seeker seems to be the fastest growing of the six systems. We have used the MindMaker6™ with hundreds of employees and managers throughout the country, and we've discovered you can expect to see more and more new workers holding these values.

So What?

MindMaker6™ authors Adams and Lynch say, "In the late 20th century, the importance of values and beliefs has weighed heavier and heavier in our understanding of how to manage, how to hire, how to teach and educate. . . ."[29] Forty years ago, workplace values were a pretty simple issue because of homogeneity. Basically, all of the workers whose opinions were valued were Loyalists and a sprinkling of Achievers who tended to take leadership roles. In the eighties, the huge influx of Involver values—carried primarily by the sixties generation—dramatically changed the way we run U.S. companies. Involver values contributed to the flattening of the organization chart, participative management, employee-involvement programs, affirmative action, and a plethora of policies and programs.

The information age and high technology also brought significant numbers of Choice-Seekers into the workplace.

We believe the most prevalent values systems among the twentysomething workforce, listed in rank order by size, are:

1. Achiever
2. Involver
3. Choice-Seeker

The bottom line: there are more diverse values than ever before among today's entry-level workers. Developing a clear understanding of values, and how to adapt your leadership style to match worker values, will be one of the key tools of the successful manager in the 1990s and beyond. Chapter nine will give you more information about varying your leadership style based on employee values.

What One Smart Business School Is Doing

Corporate leaders are troubled by the self-orientation they find in the latest crop of MBA's. In Denver, one such leader is committed to doing something about it. Bill Daniels, known as the father of cable television, has put $10 million into an MBA program at the University of Denver which emphasizes integrity, communication, community service, warmth, and commitment. Viewed with a MindMaker6™

filter, the MBA program at the University of Denver invites students to experience Involver and Loyalist values.

While their program covers the basics, such as finance and accounting, it also places a high priority on social responsibility. Weekdays are spent not only in the classroom, but out meeting minority business owners and sitting in on nonprofit board meetings. On a typical Saturday afternoon the students fix up temporary shelters for the homeless or clean up parks. Theresa Pruitt, a student who chose Denver over Stanford, speaks from her mix of Achiever, Loyalist, and Involver values: "We have to learn to work together and to help other people in order to get anywhere. To be successful, you have to learn how to work hard, too. And being successful means being able to work with other people effectively. So it is no longer *me* at all. It is *we* definitely."[30]

A recent radio broadcast by Leslie Dalkemper, a reporter for KCFR, a National Public Radio affiliate, spotlighted the Denver program. According to Dalkemper, the "effort is a response from business and educators to the avarice eighties, a time when junk bond kings ruled, and their subjects, investors, were swindled. Respect in the business world was associated with power and money, and the bigger the better. Applications to business schools across the country skyrocketed." With Wall Street's crash in 1987, business and education were forced to examine their values. Dalkemper concludes, "Time will tell whether other MBA schools will follow Denver's attempt to inject idealism into the sometimes cutthroat world of business."[31]

This chapter has begun to uncover the diversity of this twentysomething generation. Its values are not uncomplicated. In chapter four, you will delve further into *differences*—in the economy and the workforce.

TAKING ACTION

Here's how you can use what you've learned about values in this chapter to be a more successful leader:

- *Understand your employees' values.*
  The better you understand what motivates an employee, the better you'll be at improving his/her productivity and effectiveness. How do you uncover an employee's values? We have three suggestions:

  1. Spend time getting to know her and what makes her tick.

  2. Ask him what he liked about his last job, or what he didn't like, or what his ideal job would be. His answers will tell you a lot about his values. For example, if he tells you what he liked about his last job were the relationships, the committee work, and the humane atmosphere, your best guess is that his values are primarily Involver. If he tells you what he disliked about the last job were that the pace was too slow, he wasn't given the rewards he earned, and there was too much emphasis on people issues, you're probably dealing with Achiever values.

  3. Pick up a copy of *The Book of Questions,* published by Workman Publishing Company, and spend informal time with your staff grappling with some of the questions. This small, inexpensive paperback offers over 200 questions (no answers are included) that stimulate discussion and challenge values and morals. Here's what author Gregory Stock has to say about the book: "Here is an enjoyable way to find out more about yourself and others, and to confront ethical dilemmas in a concrete rather than an abstract form."[32]

- *Don't expect them to change their values.*
  For the most part, people's values remain constant through-

out their lives. We once had a manager in a seminar who asked, "When are these kids going to grow up to be Loyalists?" Waiting for young workers to change their values could be a lifelong project. Sorry.

· *Learn to see their values positively.*
Learn to see the gifts your young workers have to offer. Here's a challenge. Quickly review this chapter and find five strengths the twentysomething worker brings to the job:

1. _____

2. _____

3. _____

4. _____

5. _____

Notes

1. Alexander W. Astin, Kenneth C. Green, William S. Korn, *The American Freshman: Twenty Year Trends*, Cooperative Institutional Research Program, American Council on Education, University of California, Los Angeles.
2. American Council on Education (flyer), "New Report Tracks 20 Year Shift in Freshman Attitudes, Values and Life Goals," Higher Education Research Institute, University of California, Los Angeles, 320 Moore Hall, Los Angeles, CA 90024.
3. David Gelman, "A Much Riskier Passage," *Newsweek*, Special Edition: The New Teens, Summer/Fall. 1990.
4. Astin, Green, and Korn, *The American Freshman: Twenty Year Trends*.
5. Mark Mayfield, "Kids Fret Yet Don't Save for College," *USA Today*, June 19, 1989.
6. Astin, Green, and Korn, *The American Freshman: Twenty Year Trends*.
7. Ibid.
8. "Students Rate Salary Top Priority, Survey Says," *Denver Post*, January 12, 1991.
9. Gary Massaro, "Baby Busters: New Breed Breaks Out of Corporate Mold," *Rocky Mountain News*, November 21, 1988, p. 52.
10. Alison Leigh Cowan, "More 'Boomerang Kids' Want to Share Folks' Nest," *Arizona Daily Star*, March 12, 1989.

CHAPTER-AT-A-GLANCE

• Values make up the essence of our personal philosophy and govern the way we operate in our lives.

• Each individual has a unique set of values. However, generations historically develop widespread, pervasive belief systems.

• The eight core values of baby busters are:

1. They are self-oriented.
2. They feel cynical.
3. They are materialistic.
4. Their adolescence is extended.
5. They want quantity time.
6. They want to have fun.
7. They are slow to commit.
8. They don't bow to authority.

• Young workers tend to have a gloomy outlook, feeling paralyzed by the problems confronting the United States. Social scientists have dubbed them the "why bother?" generation.

• Five influences shaped today's young workers: parenting, declining numbers, economic turbulence, instant knowledge, and stress.

• Their behavior is driven by six values systems: Kinsperson, Loner, Loyalist, Involver, Achiever, and Choice-Seeker.

• The most prevalent values systems among the twentysomethings in rank order are: Achiever, Involver, Choice-Seeker.

• The values of this generation are more diverse than any other generation's. Developing a clear understanding of values, and how to adapt your management style to match worker values, will be one of the key tools for successful leadership in the 1990s.

---

11. Ibid.
12. Jean Davies Okimoto and Phyllis Jackson Stegall, *Boomerang Kids,* Pocket Books, 1987.
13. Massaro, p. 52.

14. Mary Anne Dolan, "Rich Is Best and Greed Still the Way to Get There," *Rocky Mountain News,* February 3, 1988.
15. American Council on Education, "1988 Freshman Survey Results," Higher Education Research Institute, University of California, Los Angeles, California 90024.
16. "Making Sense of the Sixties," a series on the Public Broadcasting System, January 22, 1991.
17. "Young Adults Wake to War Realities," *USA Today,* February 18, 1991.
18. Ibid.
19. David M. Gross and Sophronia Scott, "Proceeding with Caution," *Time,* July 16, 1990, p. 58.
20. Ibid.
21. "Students Rate Salary Top Priority, Survey Says."
22. American Council on Education (flyer), "New Report Tracks 20 Year Shift in Freshman Attitudes, Values and Life Goals."
23. "A Generation's Philosophy, Fears," *USA Today,* February 18, 1991.
24. Anastasia Toufexis, "Our Violent Kids," *Time,* June 12, 1989, p. 52.
25. Gross and Scott, p. 58.
26. David Gelman, "A Much Riskier Passage," *Newsweek,* Special Edition: The New Teens, Summer/Fall, 1990.
27. Claire Raines, "Personal Value Systems," *Journal of the Association of Operating Room Nurses,* August 1988, Vol. 48, No. 2.
28. Ibid.
29. Kenneth L. Adams and Dudley Lynch, MindMaker6™, Brain Technologies Corporation.
30. KCFR News Report: "New MBA Program at DU." Reporter: Leslie Dalkemper.
31. Ibid.
32. Gregory Stock, Ph.D., *The Book of Questions,* Workman Publishing, 1987.

Diversity allows each of us to contribute in a special way, to make our special gift a part of the corporate effort.

—Max DePree
Leadership Is an Art

It's a small world after all . . .

—Walt Disney

4

The Rainbow Coalition at Work

Give Jesse Jackson credit for a particularly pithy phrase, "the rainbow coalition." It describes the diverse population of races, colors, and cultures he hoped would sweep him into the White House in his 1988 presidential bid. Jackson's campaign phrase caught the imagination of Americans everywhere, and we think it's an apt title for this chapter on the growing diversity of workers in the United States as we approach the turn of the century.

By the year 2000, the workforce will be much different than it is today. New trends, documented by the U.S. Department of Labor, show that minorities and women will comprise the larger share of new entrants into the labor force. Thus, managing diversity will be the new challenge of the 1990s if American business hopes to create stable work environments for employees and those who manage them. According to *Fortune,* "Most of the new hires will be women or African-American, Hispanic, and Asian men. Companies that can't learn to attract the best from these groups will face a shrinking pool of desirable employees."[1]

According to the authors of *Workforce America,* while some companies are choosing to view this growing diversity in the American workforce as a problem, "leading-edge organizations see it as a means of enhancing their recruitment, marketing, and customer service efforts."[2]

In this chapter you will follow the rainbow coalition at work. Who will make up this coalition? How will you attract, train, motivate, and keep them? We'll also explore the role of women in the changing workplace, and spell out actions you can take to prepare for the rainbow coalition at work.

The Shifting Economy

Let's begin by examining a major paradigm shift as our economy switches from one driven by manufacturing to one driven by service. Watch the morning television news on just about any day of the week, and you'll be reminded of Bob Dylan's prophetic words from the sixties, ". . . oh, the times they are a-changin'." We live in an extraordinary time. Before our eyes, world politics shift from decades of despotism to overnight opposition to the status quo. The Berlin Wall is demolished into souvenir-size chunks of stone to the patriotic singing of *Deutschland Über Alles* under a single German flag. Rumanian rulers topple and communism collapses. War erupts in the Persian Gulf. All of these are signs of major shifts in fundamental societal models, or *paradigm shifts*. These are changes in the ways governments govern and societies define themselves.

No less a paradigm shift is under way in the United States. While our shift is not an overthrow of a government or despot, it is certainly as significant in its impact on every working American. We are shifting from a manufacturing paradigm, in which our society is driven by the production of goods, to a paradigm driven by the service and support of goods manufactured elsewhere. Where manufacturing produced some 30 percent of all goods and services in 1955, and 21 percent in 1985, its share will drop to less than 17 percent by year 2000, according to the Department of Labor's projections.

Three-fourths of all the jobs in the United States today are not in the manufacturing sector; instead, they are in the service industry. But "service employers who do not offer their employees oppor-

AMERICAN GOODS & SERVICES MANUFACTURED IN THE U.S.

1955	*1985*	*2000*
30%	21%	17%

tunities for growth may end up with unfilled positions or workers who don't care about their jobs."[3] This shift will bring about profound changes in the way people work, how they work, and where they work.

Additionally, of the fastest-growing job categories identified by the Department of Labor, all except service occupations will require more than the median level of education. Obviously, those who take entry-level jobs are among the most poorly trained and lowest paid employees in a business. Thus, the entry-level position has become a self-fulfilling prophecy. It's where you start when you don't have the skills and knowledge to do another, higher-paying kind of work. Traditionally, entry-level jobs have attracted the young, Anglo-American male high school graduate. The American workforce is transforming from one which is predominately white and male to Jackson's rainbow coalition. Early in this decade the effect will be felt throughout American business. The dearth of workers of this description will force increased reliance on minorities and immigrants to fill the gap.

If Dylan was right—and we think he was—there are some challenging times ahead for today's managers. They will have to learn to manage people with diverse cultural, racial, and social backgrounds. And they will have to cope with a less well-educated and trained workforce.

Of course, American business has known about the training and education gap for some time, and has tried various ways of remedying it. Most leading corporations have tuition reimbursements to encourage workers to further their education. Some companies even provide paid time off for employees finishing degrees. In most companies, there is paid time off for training. The use of in-house seminars and workshops is an increasing trend for employers who want to bring information and innovative interpersonal experiences to their workers. In fact, some $25 billion a year is spent by American businesses to bring new employees up to standard.

It's clear that this trend will continue, and that managers must be prepared to offer educational opportunities to young workers, particularly minorities, in order to create and retain effective, successful employees. Managing the rainbow coalition workforce of tomorrow will require more than just a simple understanding of the demographic and ethnic changes taking place. Waves of immigrants to the United States, particularly from Mexico, Central and South America, and Asia, will begin to fill the void in entry-level jobs as baby boomers age. African-Americans, Asian-Americans, and Hispanics will be competing for service sector jobs. These are the new individuals you'll be leading.

The smart manager will understand that she or he must do more than simply advertise for workers. To attract and keep these young workers, companies must open educational and training opportunities. "With fewer new young workers entering the workforce, employers will be hungry for qualified people and more willing to offer jobs and training to those they have traditionally ignored."[4]

A better understanding of and appreciation for plurality in the workplace will become an absolute necessity as today's manager works with tomorrow's employee. Therefore, we think it's worthwhile to take a look beyond the stereotypes and gain some insight into the expanding multiethnic workplace.

African-Americans

The 1980s were a pivotal decade for African-Americans. For the first time in history, an African-American was a viable contender for the Presidential nomination, the first African-American governor (Douglas Wilder of Virginia) was elected to office, and the first African-American (Major General Colin Powell) was appointed chairman of the Joint Chiefs of Staff and commanded all coalition forces in the Persian Gulf War. Still, these important "firsts" happened against a backdrop of increasing racial tension, crime, unemployment, and drug abuse. Then again, the media and Hollywood deserve their share of blame for exploiting and sensationalizing the negative elements in the African-American community. As Edward Lewis, publisher of *Essence,* reminds us, "More whites use cocaine and more whites live in poverty. All blacks are not on drugs. Progress is being made. Blacks do have money."[5]

Indeed, America's 31 million African-Americans are a large and diverse population. The upscale family, making $50,000 a year or more, grew to represent 13 percent of the African-American community in 1988, leaving a widening gap between the "haves" and "have nots." The most concentrated populations live in dense urban centers, and one out of every three African-American householders is under thirty-five years of age.

Undoubtedly, the biggest challenge facing these young workers is the gap in their education and skills. Forty percent drop out of high school and take jobs (if they can find them) that yield them less than $9,000 a year. A mere 13 percent in the twenty-five to thirty-four age group have earned a college degree.

Those African-Americans who enroll in college often share a background radically different from their Anglo-American peers. Eugene DeLoalich, dean of the School of Engineering at Morgan State University in Baltimore, describes the typical African-American freshman: "He lives in a household with four to six other people. Almost half are from single parent households. His family income is between $20,000 and $23,000. His parents want him to go to college but he needs a job."[6]

Hispanics

Some of us carry around the notion that young Hispanics are all impoverished immigrants recently arrived in the United States. Demographic and census reports show us this idea is patently untrue. Hispanics, like African-Americans, are diverse among themselves, with distinct cultural, racial, and linguistic differences. Made up of people who can trace their origins to Mexico, Puerto Rico, Cuba, Central and South America, many speak both English and Spanish. However, of those born in the United States, approximately 90 percent speak English perfectly, while knowing little or no Spanish themselves.

Like African-Americans, the affluent segment of this population is growing. More than 2.6 million live in households making $50,-000 and up, and most achieve this high standard of living through multiple paychecks. Affluent Hispanics are most likely to be young adults, which reflects the younger age structure of their population in general.

Unfortunately, young Hispanics experience the same crisis in education as young African-Americans. According to the Joint Committee of Congress, an overwhelming 50 percent drop out of high school and take menial labor jobs. With education a powerful factor in obtaining affluence, and affluence being identified as important to all young workers, businesses and managers have their work cut out for them. Consider the following statistics released by the U.S. Bureau of Census in 1989:

> Compared to 76 percent of U.S. adults over 25 who had completed high school and the 20 percent who had completed four or more years of college, among Hispanics, only 51 percent had completed high school and only 9 percent had four or more years of college.

Asian-Americans

Perhaps one of the most confusing forms of racial stereotypes is that which is overly positive and puts undue pressure on individuals. Asian-Americans certainly fall into this category, with many of us believing that Korean, Chinese, Japanese, and Vietnamese people are all high academic achievers, hard workers, scientifically minded, and highly competitive.

One thing is for certain: the Asian-American and Pacific Island populations are among the fastest growing in the United States. In Texas, in the period 1980 to 1985, this ethnic population grew by 67 percent. Rapid growth means that in this decade the Asian-American population nationwide is projected to grow by more than 40 percent. (The Hispanic population is expected to grow by 38.6 percent, African-Americans by 14.6 percent, and Anglo-Americans by only 3.2 percent.) The chart below shows the skyrocketing growth rate for Asian-Americans in the U.S.:

ASIAN-AMERICAN POPULATION GROWTH IN THE U.S.

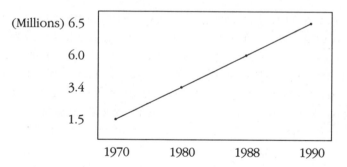

Source: U.S. Bureau of Census

California, by far, has the largest population of Asian-Americans, followed by Hawaii, New York, and Texas.

When it comes to education, Asian-Americans enjoy the highest percentage of high school and college graduates in the country. Compare them (below) with other rainbow-coalition populations.

Statistics serve one function, but rarely do they bring the picture down to the individual. The assumptions an employer may make about a worker who is Asian-American may cause a series of unfair expectations. Take the case of sixteen-year-old Sun Park, a Korean-

HIGH SCHOOL AND COLLEGE COMPLETION

	Asian-Americans	Anglo-Americans	African-Americans	Hispanics
High School Diplomas	78%	77%	63%	51%
College Degrees	33	21	11	9

Source: U.S. Bureau of Census

American. She noted that her Anglo-American peers "had this idea, probably from TV and movies, that all Asians are nerds and all Asians are smart. . . . Having a reputation for brains is nice, I guess, but it can also be a pain. They [my parents] want me to be number one. Sometimes I just like to be lazy."[7]

Thus, as a manager dealing with young Asian-Americans in the workplace, you may need to be prepared for an individual to rebel against these statistical assumptions of high standards and demand to be treated with the same expectations as his or her peers.

Women

Completing this diverse new pool of employees are women, who now make up almost half of the American workforce. If this seems less than front-page news to you, consider the following statements:

"Almost two-thirds of the new entrants into the workforce will be women."[8]

"Women's share of the labor force will grow to 47 percent."[9]

"While American business grew accustomed to women in the 1980s, during the next decade it will have to accommodate their power."[10]

In a much-publicized article for the *Harvard Business Review,* Felice N. Schwartz, president of Catalyst, Inc., a research firm dealing with women's employment, explains why "business needs all the talented women it can get."[11] Emphasizing the shrinking labor pool, Schwartz reminds us that the swollen recruitment pool created by the tidal wave of baby boomers was a never-to-be-repeated phenomenon. The days of employers having their pick of the best and brightest Anglo-American males are long gone. "Over the past decade," she notes, "the increase in the number of women graduating from leading universities has been much greater than the increase in the total number of graduates, and these women are well represented in the top 10 percent of their classes."[12]

Her claims are well-supported by a twenty-year study of college freshmen (*The American Freshman: Twenty Year Trends,* by Astin, Green, and Korn, The American Council on Education, UCLA, 1987) which documents the changing goals and aspirations of young American women. There has been a drastic shift away from such traditionally feminine career choices as teaching, nursing, and social work, into business, law, science, and engineering. More and more women are pursuing advanced degrees. Young women, in general, endorse the traditional male goals of materialism and power. Job equality is an assumed commodity. The once common view of woman as homemaker is widely rejected. "Indeed," concurs Professor Astin, "the most dramatic changes in all the freshman data since 1966 are those that reflect the effects of the Women's Movement and the changing role of women in American society."[13]

But, even with this convincing documentation, we think it's interesting to note that many young women today give little conscious thought to the terms "women's movement" and "feminist movement." Having grown up enjoying the positive results of their own mothers' battles over equal opportunity, they take for granted the educational and employment doors now open to them. Speaking for much of her generation, nineteen-year-old Yong Sin Kim, studying for both a professional music program and an MBA, says, "It's not that we don't consider feminism important; it's just that we don't see the inequality as much right now."[14]

What these young women *will* hold in common with their sisters and mothers and grandmothers as they enter the workforce is the impact of marriage and children on their careers. They will discover, along with their employers, that the struggle between baby and briefcase, between family commitments and career commitments, is intense and complicated. Nowhere was this more dramatically evident than in the moving U.S. media coverage of soldier moms leaving husbands and children to serve in the Persian Gulf. With over 52 percent of women with children under the age of six employed, compared with only 11 percent in 1960, the key word for both women and American business in the coming decade will be *flexibility*.

Felice N. Schwartz describes this flexibility simply as "the freedom to take time off."[15] She warns employers that "the price you must pay to retain the high-performing career and family woman is threefold: you must plan for and manage maternity, you must provide the flexibility that will allow them to be maximally productive, and you must take an active role in helping to make family support and high quality, affordable child care available to all women."[16]

In addition to child care, women (in fact, all potential employees) will competitively seek out jobs with such benefits as maternity/ paternity leave, elder care, job sharing, flextime, new tax deductions, and flexible health/life insurance packages. We will see an increase in job sharing, part-time workers, temporary workers, and contract workers to accommodate those with family obligations. These changes will be necessary to support a workforce soon filled to three-quarters by working parents who will be willing to trade off salary and promotion promises for benefits and protection.

If these prospects seem somewhat strange or foreboding to managers, consider some of the possible benefits in employing parents in the workforce. Nan Stone, in her article "Mother's Work," explains the highly desirable qualities many parents bring to their jobs, such as "consistency, clarity, and structure; the limits to 'because I said so' styles of authority; self-discipline and the ability to temper (their) own wants for the sake of common needs; the benefits of a long-term view, of constancy."[17]

The nineties will demand of leaders and their organizations a genuine commitment to valuing and maximizing diversity. Many companies state brave words about the value of diversity in the workplace; however, few of them translate those brave words into deeds. Here are four companies that are taking this issue seriously.

Levi Strauss

A recent *Harvard Business Review* article highlighted Levi Strauss's exceptional commitment to pluralism. As a company, Levi Strauss operates from a set of values spelled out in the corporate *Aspirations Statement*. The paragraph on diversity makes that commitment absolutely clear to every employee:

> What type of leadership is necessary to make our Aspirations a Reality? *Diversity:* Leadership that values a diverse workforce (age, sex, ethnic group, etc.) at all levels of the organization, diversity in experience, and diversity in perspectives. We have committed to taking full advantage of the rich backgrounds and abilities of all our people and to promoting a greater diversity in positions of influence. Differing points of view will be sought; diversity will be valued and honesty rewarded, not suppressed.[18]

What makes the difference at Levi Strauss & Co. is a determination to practice what they preach. In 1985, a handful of mid-level minority and women managers asked to meet with chairman Robert D. Haas. The company was not "walking its talk," they reported. Although Levi's equal opportunity record was better than virtually any other corporation's, this group was confronting "invisible barriers" interfering with advancement.

Haas organized an off-site retreat. Each of ten minority and woman managers was paired with a male Anglo-American senior manager. Together, they explored the issue of equal opportunity at Levi—sometimes painfully. After nearly three days of discussion, the senior managers agreed: "considerable unconscious discrimination" still existed.[19] They realized that equal employment opportunity requires more than numbers—that, in fact, it relies on attitudes. They decided more needed to be done.

Over the next three years, Levi held sixteen similar sessions. In 1987, the executive management committee began holding monthly forums for groups of about twenty employees. These forums have given birth to a number of initiatives, including career-development courses, support networks, and seminars.

LensCrafters

This $600 million company—with the famous slogan "Custom-Crafted Eyeglasses in About an Hour"—has made a strong commitment to the value of the individual, and recognizes diversity as essential to its success. Ban Hudson, chief executive officer of the firm's parent company, U.S. Shoe Corporation, shares LensCrafters' perspective on diversity in their workforce:

> As a company, we exist in an environment that is characterized by diversity. Our suppliers, customers, and the communities in which we operate are comprised of people representing a mix of cultures, colors, religions, ages, handicaps, experiences, interests and talents. Our effectiveness in interfacing with and satisfying the needs of those diverse individuals and groups is enhanced when the makeup of our organization reflects that environment.

Marriott

Marriott has developed special networks to increase job success among new minority workers. Job coaches are assigned to work with new hires, checking in with them on a daily basis. Coaches work with four to six workers, "answering questions, explaining procedures, and discussing any adjustment problems posed by the new work situation."[20] The relationship often lasts a few months, until the new worker feels at home on the job.

Aetna Life and Casualty

Aetna Life and Casualty in Hartford, Connecticut has hired more than a thousand workers in the past few years through a partnership between education and local organizations. Since the focus of the partnership is on improving reading and writing skills, Aetna finds this a valuable labor pool.[21]

If all this information seems overwhelming, it's helpful to keep in mind that the new diversity in the workplace will have a positive effect on many areas of American business. "If the labor shortage is handled well . . . the nineties could turn out to be a golden opportunity for African-Americans, Hispanics, high school dropouts, and others who have not shared in the American dream. If they can be prepared for the needs of tomorrow's workforce, there will be less poverty, crime, and dependence on welfare."[22]

TAKING ACTION

Here are some suggestions for preparing yourself and your company to work with the rainbow coalition:

1. Construct a demographic profile of the workers in your firm. Your employee relations or personnel department should be able to do this for you.

2. With a clear picture of your company's rainbow coalition, consider offering "plurality training" to your management group. This training, which explores and clarifies the values, concerns, beliefs, and world views of other races, sexes, and cultures, can help enlighten your managers. You will be able to decrease and hopefully eliminate the occurrence of sexist and racist language and destructive ethnic humor. Remember, as long as a single employee feels he or she is the victim of sexual or racial harassment, you are faced with the threat of legal action against your company.

3. Use the MindMaker6™ instrument mentioned in chapter three to gain a clear understanding of the values that drive your workforce.[23] Help your managers appreciate the contributions each value system brings to the work environment.

4. Set aside a day or two each year for your company to recognize the cultural diversity represented in the workforce. One federal branch holds an "International Week" every year. Persons of foreign birth wear their country's costumes. Food from different races and cultures is offered in the cafeteria. Informative videos and posters reinforce the idea of the richness in workforce diversity.

5. Have an open door policy—one without repercussions—and then check to make sure the policy is carried out. Find out if your employees believe it's safe to speak up. Many companies

have a written open door policy, but in reality the culture does
not value diverse opinions.

Notes

1. *Fortune,* September 1988, p. 46.
2. Marilyn Loden, *Workforce America,* BusinessOne-Irwin, 1991, p. 164.
3. Diane Crispell, "Workers in 2000," *American Demographics,* March 1990, p. 38.
4. *Workforce 2000: Work and Workers for the 21st Century,* U.S. Department of Labor, 1987, p. 114.
5. Judith Waldrop, "Shades of Black," *American Demographics,* September, 1990, p. 30.
6. Ibid, p. 32.
7. *Newsweek,* Summer/Fall 1990, Special Edition, p. 62.
8. *Workforce 2000,* p. 88.
9. Diane Crispell, "Workers in 2000," *American Demographics,* p. 36.
10. Sabin Russell, "Women's Growing Role in the Workplace," *San Francisco Chronicle,* October 1989, p. 11.
11. Felice N. Schwartz, "Management Women and the New Facts of Life," *Harvard Business Review,* January/February 1989, p. 68.
12. Ibid.
13. Ibid., p. 2.
14. "Twentysomething," *Newsweek,* July 16, 1990.
15. Schwartz, "Management Women and the New Facts of Life," p. 72.
16. Ibid.
17. Nan Stone, "Mother's Work," *Harvard Business Review,* September/October 1989, p. 56.
18. Robert Howard, "Values Make the Company," *Harvard Business Review,* September/October 1990, pp. 133–144.
19. Ibid., p. 135.
20. *Workforce America,* p. 168.
21. Ibid., p. 170.
22. *Denver Post,* Sunday, May 7, 1989.
23. MindMaker6™ values assessment instruments may be ordered from Bradford, Inc., 129 W. 10th Avenue, Denver, CO 80204, (303) 892-0544.

CHAPTER-AT-A-GLANCE

- Minorities and women will comprise the larger share of new entrants into the labor force by the year 2000. Managing diversity will be the new challenge of the nineties if American business hopes to create stable work environments for employees and their leaders.

- We are experiencing a paradigm shift in America, a major shift in a fundamental societal model, from a manufacturing paradigm driven by the production of goods to a paradigm driven by the service and support of goods manufactured elsewhere.

- Managers must be prepared to offer educational opportunities to young workers, particularly minorities, in order to create and retain effective, successful employees.

- Smart managers will understand that they must do more than simply advertise for workers. They must provide education and training opportunities for the rainbow coalition workforce.

- A better understanding of pluralism and the multiethnic workplace of African-Americans, Hispanics, Asian-Americans, and women will become an absolute necessity for today's manager.

- Guaranteeing success among new minority and women workers may require creative approaches. Companies such as Levi Strauss, LensCrafters, Marriott, and Aetna Life and Casualty value diversity in their corporate cultures.

*Hell, I'm in the business of building cars—not
teaching remedial math!*

—Lee Iacocca

5

Workforce 2000: A Report Card

The chairman of Chrysler Corporation had better get used to the
idea: Corporate America is going to have to teach the three R's. Why?
It's simple. As we've already noted, the workforce is shrinking and
becoming increasingly diverse. Add the fact that today's high
schools are not equipping graduates with many practical, useful,
job-related skills and we have what former Education Secretary
Laura Cavazos calls "a national tragedy."[1]

The twentysomething generation is entering an economy in
which more and more occupations require higher skills and educational levels. The U.S. Department of Labor notes that among the
fastest growing jobs, the trend toward higher educational requirements is striking. Of all the new jobs created between 1984 and 2000,
more than half will require some education beyond high school, and
almost one-third will demand college graduates. The good jobs of
the future will go to those who have the training to enable them to
be productive in a skill-driven, service economy. If they aren't learning these skills in our educational system, then American businesses
will have to step up to the task.

The implications for American business are significant. The major
source of skilled and unskilled labor in the coming decade will be
these undereducated, untrained, and untested high school graduates, one-half of whom will not go on to attend college. *U.S. News
and World Report* calls them "the forgotten half," and comments

that, "in the upcoming decade, the economy will depend as much on this diverse group of less schooled workers as it will on the nation's software programmers and rocket scientists."[2]

In this chapter we explore what's going to happen to the baby busters as they move through our educational system and begin to enter the job market. We also examine the skills shortfall and give you examples of what some American businesses are doing to aid their unskilled workers. Finally, we offer some concrete steps you can take to begin closing the training gap yourself.

Skills and Education

Exactly what are we talking about when we refer to a "skills short-fall" which seemingly implicates our own educational system? Here are some startling facts to grapple with:

- The National Science Foundation and the Department of Education recently commissioned an international study in which American teenagers came in dead last in math and well below the mean in science. They were outscored across the board by students from four other countries and four Canadian provinces.[3]
- "A recent study by the University of Texas concluded that 26 million adult Americans are functionally illiterate, meaning they can't read or write well enough to fill out a job application or do enough arithmetic to count change."[4]
- A U.S. Department of Education study of young people concluded that only one-quarter of Anglo-Americans, 7 percent of Hispanics, and 3 percent of African-Americans could decipher a bus schedule.[5]

If this isn't enough to give you tremors, consider several more factors that complicate the situation. Those students who do succeed in high school and opt for a college education are taking longer to complete their degree programs. On the average, a young person now spends five years earning a BA degree, compared to the mean time of 4.5 years in 1972. This delayed entry into the workforce comes at the very time when more entry-level workers are needed. Whatever the problems in secondary and higher education, one fact is clear: jobs in today's economy require increasingly higher skill levels, and those entering the workforce, especially in the service sector, are the young workers who have the least amount of education and experience.

Who Is to Blame?

An obvious question follows this discussion: Who is to blame for this abysmal situation? Our schools? Parents? The young people themselves? Society at large? Opinion is divided, but those who fault the schools are forthcoming with their criticism. In its June 26, 1989, cover story, *U.S. News and World Report* stated, "Survey after survey shows that teachers and guidance counselors rank securing a job for students as their last priority," and further noted that, "Instead of receiving useful training and counseling, noncollege-bound youths typically end up in general-education and vocational courses . . . little more than corrals for handicapped students, minorities and kids with discipline problems."[6]

A young Hispanic student, Reynaldo, seems to agree: "Why bother, man? You go and sit all day in those classrooms and when you come out you don't have anything more than you went in with. I know the teachers try, but what's the point? Do I really need to sit in a class in social studies? I already know I'm a minority and that we're poor. What I want to know is how to make some money so I can buy the things I want. Give me a class on making money fast and I'll be there every day!" Although he laughs good-naturedly, Reynaldo may be speaking for a large number of minority students who fail to see the relevance of much of what they learn in today's classroom. For these young people—the "why bother?" generation—high school and even college seem to be years to be endured with no real practical outcome.

Another complicating factor is the *type* of course work students, even university students, are pursuing. According to Harvard professor Robert Reich, what the American worker needs is an ability to define problems, gather data, conceptualize and reorganize information, make conclusions, test them, discuss findings with coworkers, create teams that generate options, and then persuade others.[7] These are the sort of skills students are most likely to get from course work in the humanities, where they examine how others have struggled with similar challenges through the ages. Subjects like philosophy, literature, history, and anthropology offer the best preparation for much that will happen on the job. Unfortunately, these are just the classes the majority of students are avoiding today. Instead, they're flocking to computer and business courses.

The Two-Minute Mind

Educational psychologist Jane Healy takes a different view of the situation. She blames busy parents and television for what she calls the "two-minute mind." In an article for *Contemporary Magazine,* Healy gives us three potential reasons for such a development.

The minds of our children, she says, have been "nourished on the rapid-fire, frenetic images of TV, especially 'Sesame Street,' or on video games that may help hand-to-eye coordination but do little to improve language and analytical thinking skills." She further comments that these impressionable beings are "living in homes where adults are too busy to talk with them, instead of at them." Finally, she faults the classrooms of today, where "instead of learning by interacting with educators and other students, they're stuck at desks, silently scribbling on worksheets. . . ."[8]

Healy warns us that unless we want young people who cannot concentrate on anything that doesn't come packaged in a two-minute segment, we must turn off the TV, talk to our children, read to them, and help them to reason. The results would surely show themselves in the future workplace, with a new generation of skilled, communicative, thinking workers.

A Manager Speaks Out

Marlene is a thirty-eight-year-old manager in the billing department for a health maintenance organization (HMO) in Omaha. She supervises a staff of eight, four of whom are between twenty-one and twenty-six. "I don't understand it," she says. "These kids should know what to do, but I find I spend a lot of time covering the basics with them. Of the four, two are college graduates, and the other two came to us from one of the community colleges in the area. They can't do even simple calculations for our members' accounts if the computer happens to go down. How did they graduate?"

The frustration Marlene expresses is felt by many managers we've talked with throughout the country. If their perceptions are accurate, a sizable portion of today's young workforce seems to lack the fundamental skills needed to be successful in their jobs. When the New York Telephone Company gave its basic employment test in fundamental skills in math, reading, and problem-solving to 57,000 employees in 1986, 54,900 failed! Ninety-six percent! In addition, 70 percent of the NYTC employees who took the company's test for technical ability also failed. NYTC places the responsibility for improved training squarely upon the shoulders of its employees, who must learn on their own.[9]

In the case of Robert, a young man in his early twenties and a repairman-installer for NYTC, the self-education concept has worked. But he is clearly an exception. "My dad," he tells us, "worked for this company for nearly forty years. He started as a laborer with less than a high school education and gradually worked his way up to a manager's position by the time he retired. I have a high school diploma and I'm going to college at night on my own.

I know I have to get a degree if I want to get ahead in this company. I don't want to wait forty years like my dad did before I make manager. It's hard, but I want to move up fast. This is a good company and I want to earn more money and have more responsibility. A lot of people think it's going to be handed to them. I don't."

Clearly, Robert is different from many of the twentysomething workers we've interviewed. He is taking charge of his own future and getting the skills he needs. But what do we do about the remaining, more typical young workers who are not so motivated?

As Steve Reinemund, president of Pizza Hut, explains, "Finding competent employees is more time-consuming than any other issue we have. There are people who want jobs and we want people, but there is not a match between what we need and what they're prepared to do."[10]

Future Jobs Will Require More Education

Before we leave this discussion to talk about some solutions, consider the chart below, which compares the differences between education requirements for today's jobs and the jobs of the future that young workers will have to fill.

Today, only 22 percent of all occupations require a college degree. However, all job categories listed by the Department of Labor except one—jobs in the service sector—will require higher education and

Education Required	Current Jobs	New Jobs
8 years or less	6%	4%
1–3 years of high school	12	10
4 years of high school	40	34
1–3 years of college	20	22
4 years of college or more	22	30
Total	100%	100%
(Median years of school)	(12.8)	(13.5)

Source: Bureau of Labor Statistics

skill levels by the year 2000. When skill requirements in language, reasoning, and mathematics are averaged, only 4 percent of the new jobs can be filled by individuals with the lowest level of skills, compared to 9 percent of jobs requiring those same low skills today.[11]

Bringing School to the Worker

Obviously, the skills gap is going to have to be narrowed, if not completely filled in and patched. The reality of the situation is that corporations and businesses, both small and large, will have to take up the task of bringing school to the worker. The signs are everywhere. American businesses spend more and more each year on the training, education, and development of their workers. When one Corning Glass plant discovered 66 percent of its 20,000 employees had reading deficiencies, management decided 5 percent of all work time would be devoted to training.[12] Lee Iacocca, chairman of Chrysler Corporation, estimates his company spends in the neighborhood of $11 million annually "teaching the three R's they didn't learn in school."[13]

U.S. West

Here's how one large corporation, U.S. West, formerly part of the Bell system, is meeting the challenge. The firm employs more than 60,000 people in a fourteen-state area. A corporate study by the company found that new employees needed to be skilled in four key areas: marketing, sales, human relations, and the technological disciplines. Connie McArthur, director of human resources and strategic planning, believes demographic shifts will soon force the company to invest greater effort in training employees to become what she calls "totalists" instead of generalists or specialists.

In 1988, U.S. West began a five-year, $20 million educational program to meet the range of training requirements of its employees.

"The two most critical areas are an ability to learn quickly and good problem-solving skills, and that means math," said McArthur.[14] When a company screening test revealed an overall decline in scores in the basic skills area, U.S. West began efforts to train employees in the skills that range the gamut from early education through college, with a specific program in math, engineering, and science.

Public Service Company of Colorado

The state's largest natural gas and electricity provider, Public Service Company of Colorado, maintains a busy human-resource management department, which provides a wide range of educational and training programs for its employees. Paul Thomsen, manager of human resources, says, "We've seen a phenomenal growth in the number and variety of courses we offer to our employee population. We provide training at all levels, from remedial reading to programs in which an employee can earn a master's degree through one of the local colleges. We're going to have to do much more of this in the future."

Jeanne Boyer is the coordinator of continuing education programs at the company, organizing classes offered to employees during off-hours. Her curriculum is loaded with courses on punctuation, grammar and spelling, handling math anxiety, and business writing. "We get a lot of employee-students who need to improve the basic skills needed to do their jobs," Boyer explains. "Quite a few of them are younger workers in their twenties."

For instance, when the utility's repair shop discovered that some of the mechanics were unable to effectively read and comprehend repair manuals, a special class in remedial reading was organized to improve the reading skills of the mechanics.

"Our mission is to improve the overall education and training of the company's employees and managers," says Richard Crites, director of training and development for the utility's 6,500 employees. "Whether it's remedial classes or a college degree program, it's a fact that the company is committed to creating an educated, highly trained workforce, and it's our job to see that it happens."

Burger King

In one east coast Burger King franchise, the owner recently found himself facing all the problems we've discussed—young employees with poor language skills, a shrinking labor pool, high turnover, and escalating training costs.

After surveying other industry leaders for practical solutions, he made a courageous move. He agreed to pay for a college education for all employees who stayed on the job for four years. Two years later, his turnover has gone from 40 percent to 9 percent per year and his training costs are down 75 percent.[15]

International Initiatives

Germany

Germany has a special way for teens to earn while they learn: apprenticeships. According to a March 1991 NBC/United Airlines *In-Flight Report,* roughly 70 percent of German teens take advantage of apprenticeship programs jointly sponsored by the government, schools, and corporations. Students sixteen to nineteen years old may sign up to work with master craftsmen—chefs, engineers, and mechanics—for three years. Those years provide solid practical experience. With a high school drop-out rate of roughly 35 percent, apprenticeships offer alternatives for students. Nearly 95 percent of the apprentices are later hired as full-time employees.

A spokesperson for Siemens Corporation says, "This is an investment in the future of our youth, in our companies, and in our country." Although American companies offer nearly 850 internships—close cousins to European apprenticeships—few of them are paid, and only a small percentage turn into full-time employment.

Sweden
Susan Tifft, writing in *Agenda,* examined what's being done to close the skills gap in the European community: "Swedish schools consciously forge links between the classroom and *Arbetsliv,* or, 'the worklife.' " Beginning as early as the first grade, children have the chance to spend up to several weeks annually in factories, public agencies, and other companies. Compulsory education in Sweden ends at age sixteen. Students can then choose from up to twenty-seven educational or occupational tracks.[16]

Great Britain
In Great Britain, Tifft writes, there has been a significant increase in the need to provide basic skills education to blue-collar workers and practical skills training for white-collar workers. The Thatcher government implemented national curriculum and certification tests in 1988, and schools and community colleges are taking an active role in coordinating entry-level training for young people.[17]

It is quite possible that your company doesn't have a full-time training department like some of the bigger organizations we've mentioned. This doesn't mean you can't help your employees close gaps in their knowledge or skills. Many commercial training and development firms offer short courses on useful subjects that will enhance your employees' productivity. These classes range from a few hours of tune-up to extended, sophisticated training over a period of weeks.

The Role of Training, Education, and Development

Every manager should understand the differences between training, education, and development learning experiences. Often when a company is downsizing or finds itself in a financial squeeze, it lops off all the training activities as a cost-saving move. Such action is probably the worst mistake a company or manager can make.

Training: Skills that can be applied immediately on the job and that are measurable and/or observable.

Education: Skills that will be applied on the job at some future time. They cannot be measured or observed until the future application.

Development: Skills that are personally enriching and that enhance individuals' quality of life. They may or may not be applied directly on the job. They are often difficult to measure or observe, but are usually beneficial to program participants.

With these distinctions in mind you can see that if you have to cut anything in order to trim the budget, start with the development activities, since they have the least chance of direct application on the job and payback to the company. Next, you might need to curtail education activities because they are always future-oriented. In times of business downturns, there may not be a "future" in which to apply these skills. Finally, training should not be cut at all; to the contrary, it should be maximized. Your employees will need all the back-on-the-job, high-payoff skills they can muster to maximize productivity in times of economic hardship.

Analyze Training Needs
Some caveats: Before you choose any kind of educational experience or training program for your employees, do your homework. It is worthwhile to spend some time conducting a training-needs analysis before you spend a lot of money on some off-the-shelf program that may or may not meet your employees' learning needs. You want to match the program to a clearly defined need for either training skills, education for future job application, or personal development.

A training-needs analysis requires a careful comparison of knowledge, resources, and attitudes of your employees. Here are three key questions to consider:

1. *Do the employees have the basic skills knowledge to do what they are supposed to do?*

This question addresses the knowledge issue. Employees and their managers must have the necessary skills knowledge to perform the tasks they are assigned. If the answer to this question is "No" or "I'm not certain," then skills training may be required. What learning experiences do your employees need? Do they have trouble writing clearly, with correct grammar, punctuation, and spelling? Do they need a refresher course in mathematics? Are their interpersonal communication skills up to par? The litmus test is that the training must be immediately applicable on the job and the results must be measurable or observable.

2. *Do the employees have the necessary resources to do their jobs?*

This question addresses both physical and human resources. Are the appropriate tools and equipment available to the employee? Are there enough employees to do the work that is required and to perform with acceptable results? If the answer is "No," then your company may need to provide the required resources.

3. *If employees have the knowledge to do the work and have the necessary resources, is there still some problem with productivity?*

If the answer to this question is "Yes," then you have a behavioral problem in the workforce. The answer is not necessarily more training or resources. Instead, intensive coaching and counseling with the nonperforming employee may be needed.

Getting Expert Help

Once you've identified your needs, you'll have to choose a trainer or instructor to deliver the goods. *Be careful.* While the majority of training consultants are ethical and want to do a good job for you, it doesn't follow that all of them can perform at high skills levels. Ask for references and check them out. A reputable training firm will welcome such scrutiny.

BENEFICIAL'S TRAINING FOR NEW HIRES

The Beneficial Corporation, headquartered in Peapack, New Jersey, has just completed a multi-million-dollar entry-level training program. The eight-course program, called Beneficial Exceptional Service Training (BEST), is designed to:

1. Bring new employees up to a minimum level of productivity within two weeks. The quick start-up improves new workers' self-esteem and confidence; it also promotes better feelings among other employees since new workers carry their own weight very quickly.
2. Communicate corporate values. New employees are educated about Beneficial's values and standards of performance. When new workers are taught the tasks they will perform, they are also taught *how* to perform tasks so that standards are met and company values are communicated to customers.
3. Involve managers as coaches. Office managers—viewed at Beneficial as coaches rather than bosses—attend training that includes a section on "Managing the BEST Training Process."

The training of new hires has been so successful and so well-reviewed that long-term employees have requested the training; they didn't want to be left behind. So Beneficial has added refresher and supplemental training for existing staff as well.

Another option is to consider hiring faculty from the local community college or university to bring needed classes to your workers. Faculty members often welcome an opportunity to earn some extra money through off-hours or Saturday teaching. Their fees are likely to be negotiable and they're likely to charge less than commercial training firms. But, again, don't simply assume that by hiring a local faculty member you are getting a top-quality instructor. Be sure to check references.

A very inexpensive resource for employee training can be found in workbooks from Crisp Publications. Owner and publisher Mike Crisp has created a unique market niche for his company's books.

Each workbook is designed to be completed by an individual in about an hour's time, without the need for a formal classroom session. Low-cost workbooks such as *Better Business Writing, Successful Self-Management, Customer Satisfaction: The Other Half of Your Job, Attitude, Your Most Priceless Possession, I Got the Job!,* and many others can be used for a very cost-effective, in-house educational program. There are currently more than one hundred titles available in this series. The content is top-notch, and the packaging is attractive and nonintimidating to the adult learner.[18]

Finally, you may wish to consider putting your employees in charge of their own learning improvement. This is especially true if you are unable to completely underwrite the cost of an employee education program. Ask your workers to share the cost for workshops, evening classes, and seminars. In doing so, you can create a sense of ownership, as well as a personal investment in their own learning process.

The decade ahead will require increasing numbers of companies to follow the lead of Chrysler, U.S. West, Public Service Company of Colorado, Beneficial, and other employers who find it necessary to teach the "three R's." Although Mr. Iacocca may not like it, neither his company nor others facing the shortfall in skills and education among young American workers can afford to do less. With some creativity, commitment, and research, you can take steps toward closing the skills gap and ensuring a brighter future for you and your company.

TAKING ACTION

Here are ten diagnostic questions to ask yourself about the skills of your twentysomething employees and your company's commitment to closing the skills gap.

1. Do you know, firsthand, the educational level of each employee who you must lead?
2. Does your company have a budget set aside specifically for providing training to entry-level employees and retraining for experienced employees and managers?
3. Have you ever conducted a training-needs analysis to determine the skills employees need for maximum productivity?
4. Does your company have a full-time training department that is led and staffed by qualified training and development specialists?
5. What percent of your annual budget is devoted to training?
6. When was the last time that you, as a manager or supervisor, completed a formal training session?
7. Does your company provide support for personnel who wish to further their education in after-hours classes?
8. Does your company offer short training events such as a "Brown Bag Lunch," where employees can have lunch and experience a short learning event?
9. Is the training and retraining of employees a priority for top management?
10. What single, specific action could you initiate as a manager to begin providing needed skills training for your employees?

Notes

1. "U.S. Teens Rank Low in Math, Science," *Rocky Mountain News,* February 1, 1989.

CHAPTER-AT-A-GLANCE

- The twentysomething generation is entering an economy in which increasing numbers of occupations require higher educational and technical skills.

- The major source of skilled and unskilled labor in the coming decade will be undereducated, undertrained, and untested high school graduates, half of whom will not go on to college.

- The basic skills levels of many entry-level workers are poor. No one institution is to blame. Rather, the educational system, parents, and employers must take action to provide the training and education workers need to work productively.

- Young people have been reared by a surrogate parent—television. They have a "two-minute mind" when it comes to attention span.

- Several U.S. companies have taken action to provide remedial skills for workers who need help. American business will need to become an active partner with the educational system to close the skills gap.

- Germany, Sweden, and Britain are initiating innovative programs aimed at training young entry-level workers and retraining older workers.

- There are important differences between training, education, and development activities that companies provide to their employees. Failure to note and plan with these differences in mind can be very costly to organizations.

---

2. "The Forgotten Half," *U.S. News and World Report,* June 26, 1989, p. 45.
3. "U.S. Teens Rank Low in Math, Science."
4. Ron Zemke, "Training in the 90's," *Training,* January, 1987, p. 48.
5. *Workforce 2000: Work and Workers for the 21st Century,* U.S. Department of Labor, 1987, pp. 1102–1103.
6. "The Forgotten Half," p. 48–49.
7. Dr. Roger Selbert, *FutureScan,* November 5, 1990.
8. Diane Eicher, "The Two-Minute Mind," *Contemporary Magazine, Denver Post,* September 16, 1990, p. 12.
9. "The Forgotten Half," p. 47.

10. Ibid., p. 48.
11. *Workforce 2000,* p. 99.
12. Ibid., p. 101.
13. "Can You Compete?," *Business Week,* December 17, 1990.
14. "Workers' Skill Gap Hobbles U.S. Economic Prospects," *Denver Post,* May 7, 1989, p. 7.
15. "Ignorance of Math Poses Threat to Society," *Denver Post,* July, 9, 1989, p. 1.
16. Susan Tifft, "Ready, Willing and Able?" *Agenda,* Spring, 1991, pp. 30–31.
17. Ibid.
18. To order Crisp Publications workbooks, contact Bradford, Inc., 129 W. Tenth Avenue, Denver, CO 80204, or call (303) 896-0544.

A senior executive, evaluating some recent graduates, said (tongue in cheek), "They know everything, but not much else."

—Stephen M. Wolf
Chairman, President, and CEO
United Airlines

6

What Managers and Workers Are Saying

In this chapter, you will read six interviews. These are actual interviews, but the names and job locations have been changed so we could guarantee that you would get honest answers. We begin with three young workers, quoted verbatim. We have not corrected their grammar or word usage. This will give you an opportunity to listen to young workers' opinions about the way they were raised, about how they are different, about their dream jobs and ideal managers. We think you'll find it uncanny how much these three twentysomething workers are like the typical worker we've profiled in previous chapters.

Next, you'll meet three managers in a variety of industries in different parts of the country. We've included their names, job titles, and companies. You will be able to see how similar or different your experiences have been in managing and motivating this twentysomething generation. Finally, we'll share our interview format so you can conduct some interviews of your own.

Three Twentysomething Workers

Raynelle

Raynelle, twenty-three, is a customer-information-center representative at a consumer data company in Kansas City, Missouri. She completed two years of college before she started this job four years ago. Her previous work experience was in retail. In addition to her current job, Raynelle teaches aerobics part-time.

Q. What is your most important priority—the thing that means the most to you?

A. Family.

Q. Do you think your parents' generation were workaholics?

A. To an extent, yes. When I was younger, my mother was working and going to school at the same time. Always pushing herself to do more.

Q. Do you want your life to be different from theirs?

A. I work a lot, too, but I don't want to work as hard and get as little as they did.

Q. Would you be a different kind of parent than they were?

A. Yes. I would try to be home more for my children than my parents were able to be for me.

Q. If you could have the perfect job, what would it be like?

A. My own hours. I'd want to be my own boss. Writing fiction.

Q. How about the perfect boss?

A. Coming around maybe once a week to see how I was doing. Not hanging over my shoulder. Let me do my job and let me show you at the end of the week.

Q. What keeps your current job from being ideal?

A. Monotony.

Q. Do you feel you have the right skills for your job?

A. Yes.

Q. What's your boss like?
A. He's fair and honest. He's only a few years older than me. He's a checker, though. Checking on me a couple of times a day.

Q. If you could change one thing about him, what would it be?
A. The checking.

Q. What do you think is the very best thing about your generation? The worst?
A. The best thing is we don't seem to be as inhibited as our parents were. We're more "just go out and do it. Go for it!" The worst is there's not any leadership for my generation. There's no role models. No one's made a great impression. No Martin Luther King. No Kennedys. Even no fads or groups like the Beatles that everyone follows.

Juan

Juan is a twenty-two-year-old employee at a paint company in Minneapolis. He's had this job almost five years. As a high school student, Juan worked summers for the school district mowing grass. After completing eleventh grade, he took his current job. Originally, he was a part-time employee in the warehouse. Today he works full time making paint.

Q. Do you think your values are the same as your parents'?
A. No, they're different. They believe in getting a real good education, making it through high school and getting into college. But I believe you don't need all that education to become successful. Common sense is what you need.

Q. What is your most important priority—the thing that means the most to you?
A. Work. Because I don't have my own family.

Q. Do you think your parents' generation were workaholics?
A. Yes. My father. He's the main janitor at a high school. He calls

Saturdays, Sundays. He has people working, and he's constantly checking in. It drives me up a wall.

Q. Do you want your life to be different from theirs?
A. I don't want it to be that different. They did a good job raising five kids through hard times. My father broke his back and couldn't work for a year.

Q. Would you be a different kind of parent than they were?
A. Not really.

Q. If you could have the perfect job, what would it be like?
A. Being a fireman or a medic. Because you're helping someone else instead of making a product.

Q. How about the perfect boss?
A. There is no perfect boss. They're all the same. But my boss doesn't get too personal or work me that hard.

Q. What keeps your current job from being ideal?
A. I would like to make more money.

Q. Do you feel you have the right skills for your job?
A. Yes.

Q. What's your boss like?
A. You can talk to him. He's like a second dad.

Q. If you could change one thing about him, what would it be?
A. His temper. Make him more calm. When he loses his temper, it's something small, but there's so much pressure on him that he blows up.

Q. What do you think is the very best thing about your generation? The worst?
A. The best thing is we're young and still experimenting. Drugs are the worst thing. Without drugs, we would've been better educated—and not just about drugs.

Patty

Patty, twenty-four, works in public relations for a county recreation district in Eugene, Oregon. She's had this job a little over a year. A public-relations and marketing assistant with a bachelor's degree in journalism, Patty writes press releases and articles for employee newsletters. She writes a newsletter that goes out quarterly from the board of directors to the public. Patty coordinates and finds sponsorships for golf tournaments and other special events.

Her past work experience includes three years as assistant manager for a fabric store and free-lance work, putting together catalogues and advertisements.

Q. Do you think your values are the same as your parents'?

A. They're similar. And I'm surprised. During high school and college, I thought I'd never act this way. But, to my surprise, I am starting to come out to be very similar to my parents.

Q. What is your most important priority—the thing that means the most to you?

A. Relationships with family and friends.

Q. Do you think your parents' generation were workaholics?

A. They work all the time. When I was two, I threw a temper tantrum when the babysitter came over because I was very upset that my mother was leaving. I wanted her to stay. I wanted her to play with me, and I became very angry when she was leaving. I threw everything off my high-chair tray because she was going off to work.

Q. How do you want your life to be different from theirs?

A. I grew up wanting to become very successful, and get further than my mother had. But I'm realizing that this is very hard to do.

Q. Would you be a different kind of parent than they were?

A. I think I'll be very similar. My brothers and I are fairly successful young people, and I want to give my kids the same thing.

Q. If you could have the perfect job, what would it be like?
A. I would have my own advertising firm. And I'd be able to set my own hours. Bring my kids to work if I wanted to. I'd have lots of people working under me, so I could take all the great jobs, do all the creative and planning, and have all the other people implement all of my great ideas. I'd make oodles of money.

Q. How about the perfect boss?
A. The perfect boss is a hands-off boss. Someone who gives you directives, says, "This is the end result I want." And he or she doesn't care how you achieve it, as long as you get that end result. This would give you a lot of room for growth and a lot of room for experimentation.

Q. What keeps your current job from being ideal?
A. I want more responsibility for the types of projects I'm working on. I would want to be on salary, and I want benefits. I never thought benefits were important. Then one of my friends had to have an appendicitis, and now he's bankrupt because he had no health insurance. Health insurance is number one. Dental and eyesight is next. And a saving plan for retirement. Flexible time would be great: if you worked extra one week you could take that time off the next. Paid vacation time would be nice. There has to be some play in the workplace to make people stay.

Q. Do you feel you have the right skills for your job?
A. Most definitely. But I'd like to keep my skills current.

Q. What's your boss like?
A. Fun. Energetic. Devoted. Easy to get along with. Hands off. Pretty terrific. She's in her mid-thirties.

Q. If you could change one thing about her, what would it be?
A. She'd be in the office more. She has so many meetings sometimes it's hard to get ahold of her, like if I have to make changes.

Q. What do you think is the very best thing about your generation? The worst?

A. The best thing is that everyone seems pretty open. Everyone realizes the need for communication. Relationships are more important than work. Personal accomplishment is more important than money. The baby boomers have taken the really great jobs, leaving none or just a few for my age group to even get into and wait to move up. So we're looking for different avenues than simply money. Money's important for recreation and lifestyle, like going skiing. The worst thing is our emphasis on achieving, being our own worst enemies. That we're so motivated at doing better than our parents, and we're so motivated to achieve, which is a good trait, but if you don't, it really sets you back. It's hard to chase the baby boomers who have so much and left us so dry. Still, you have your long-range goals and your short-range goals, and when you reach them, you set another one. Sometimes it's a big responsibility.

Three Managers

Rob Schwartz, ARA Services

Rob Schwartz, thirty-seven, is regional vice president with ARA, a national food and beverage service provider. Rob, who is based in Irving, Texas, holds an MBA degree and has worked in the food service industry for sixteen years. He supervises six district managers and one secretary. ARA has been following young-worker trends for years, since the twentysomething generation is one of its leading employee suppliers.

Q. Are young workers today different from previous generations?

A. I think they are. There's less dedication to the company—and vice versa. Back when I came out of college, it was more commonplace to anticipate that you'd be with one company for a career. Young people today plan on changing companies, perhaps once a year. Ironically, we as companies tend to foster this because we hire experienced salespeople from someplace else, rather than develop our own force.

Q. Do young workers seem to have the necessary skills to do the work?

A. Yes, except communication skills, both oral and written, are lacking.

Q. Do you think young workers have different attitudes and beliefs than you?

A. Yes. They work to live, rather than live to work. They want to make money, rather than confront the challenges of the job.

Q. What is your most difficult challenge in supervising young workers?

A. Convincing them that they need to be patient and learn their jobs before they can move up the ladder. There's an anxiousness to move up in status and title that is hard to combat.

Q. Do young workers offer any unique assets to the organization?

A. Enthusiasm. Newer ideas. They don't have prior experience which tells them that they can't do something. Ironically, the very qualities that make them frustrating to work with—impatience, lack of training—in some instances allow for energy and fresh approaches.

Q. If you could change just one thing about young workers, what would it be?

A. Their lack of patience for longer-term employment. Their unwillingness to follow a development plan that would include relocation to further their careers with the company.

Q. Have you had to make any changes to adapt to the new, diverse workforce?

A. There seems to be more upfront, formal training.

Q. Can you think of a time when an approach you've taken with a twentysomething worker was less than effective?

A. The pep talk I've given to an employee who's discouraged hasn't worked every time, lately.

Q. What kinds of training do you think could benefit your young workers?

A. Communication, written and oral skills, which we have for our veteran employees. For the entry-level worker, we have a training program introducing the skills necessary for our food service industry; this training is full time for three months.

Susan Smirnoff, Ruder Finn

Susan Smirnoff, thirty-eight, is senior vice president of Ruder Finn, a public relations firm based in New York City. Susan has a BA in speech communication and has worked in public relations for nearly twenty years. Her career includes a stint as a news reporter and a job in press information with the U.S. government. She has been with Ruder Finn for twelve years, where she has a tremendous amount of exposure to twentysomething workers.

Q. Are young workers today different from previous generations?

A. In the past three years, I've noticed younger workers to be more intelligent and hardworking. A lot of this has to do with the competitiveness of the marketplace, but also with young workers genuinely wanting to excel.

Q. Do young workers seem to have the necessary skills to do the work?

A. In New York City, in a fairly sophisticated industry, the new employees are already somewhat savvy about the business world, beyond what one would expect from a recent college graduate.

Q. What is your most difficult challenge in supervising twentysomething workers?

A. One situation I had, unlike anything I'd ever experienced before, arose when one young worker was having difficulty with another, but neither could articulate what the problem was. I tried to resolve it as a matter of "chemistry," but eventually had to separate them.

Q. Do young workers offer any unique assets to the organization?
A. In this business, their innocence and lack of experience is needed to ferret out information, because they're not yet afraid of getting a big fat "no" at the other end of the line.

Q. If you could change just one thing about young workers, what would it be?
A. One guy who's twenty-five but looks twenty-two, and a lot of our clients don't take him seriously, though he's brilliant and savvy. I wish he looked older.

Q. Have you had to make any changes to adapt to the new, diverse workforce?
A. We have a new, very competitive executive training program, which helps screen employees. It began as an internship for college students, but recently was adapted to training many young workers who become part of our firm.

Q. What kinds of training do you think could benefit your young workers?
A. Writing, particularly in a communications business. Common sense, which is something you can't teach. I wish there was more university experience that offered more practical experience: memo or brief writing. I wish young workers arrived with more polished writing skills.

Q. What is your organization doing that is helpful in managing young workers?
A. We're providing free, on-the-scene education, both during the day and evening, free of charge, right here in the office, including

grammar and computer lessons. We do it after work or during an extended lunch hour. And we encourage them to participate in other education programs in the field.

Jim Shaffer, Towers Perrin

Jim, forty-three, is vice president and principal of Towers Perrin, a consulting firm in Rosslyn, Virginia. Jim has a BA in communications and political science from the University of Kansas. He spent five years as press secretary to the Governor of Kansas. He then headed up corporate communications for Blue Shield. After working for the National Safety Council, he joined Towers Perrin in 1980. Jim directly supervises three young workers and works with people of all ages in his consulting work.

Q. Are young workers today different from previous generations?

A. Absolutely. The principal difference is their value systems. They are very focused on self, or what we call the "I factor." They are interested in the quality of life, and much more oriented toward a sense of purpose than a sense of company.

Q. Do young workers seem to have the necessary skills to do the work?

A. No. But name me a single group of people who have the skills to get all the work done that needs to be done. Are there skills gaps? Yes. Educational gaps? Yes.

Q. Do you think the young workers have different attitudes and beliefs than you?

A. No. It seems the same to me. You simply have to learn to appeal to a different sense of values, and if you can do that, you can still produce energetic, excited, turned-on workers.

Q. What is your most difficult challenge in supervising your workers?

A. To constantly listen to them, day to day, in such a way that you can communicate your vision of the organization and link it to

95

their life's purpose. Then you form an alignment between their needs and your needs.

Q. Do young workers offer any unique assets to the organization?

A. Yes. A perspective that people of other generations don't have. It's important that we understand that perspective, because they are the source of new and creative ideas—and are a huge part of the market.

Q. If you could change one thing about young workers, what would it be?

A. Where they have to go to school. The American education system.

Q. Are you having any difficulty finding enough young workers to fill your entry-level jobs?

A. We don't really have entry-level jobs here. They tend to be for experienced people, but most companies aren't having trouble so much with quantity of workers as with skill matches. There are some real literacy issues out there.

Q. Have you had to make any changes to adapt to the new, diverse workforce?

A. Everyone has and will. There are far more jobs than people, and you have to be the very best at appealing to the smaller labor force. To win, you must go after the best and brightest, and you have to know how to appeal to them.

Q. Can you think of an instance when an approach you've taken with a young worker was less than effective?

A. Older people run the risk of taking themselves too seriously and have a tendency to come off as condescending, phoney, or patronizing, even when they don't mean to when dealing with younger workers. You must listen to young workers, acknowledge them and understand them. Even when they come to you with the worst ideas that have failed dozens of times, you have to listen and not say so, knowing all they need is about another ten years of experience.

Q. What is Towers Perrin doing that is helpful in managing young workers?

A. We give help through donations to educational support programs. We adopt high schools.

TAKING ACTION

Now that you've had a chance to listen to three twentysomething workers and three of their managers, you may want to run some comparisons. We highly recommend that—unless you know them so well you know all their answers already—you sit down with each of your younger workers and ask them the types of questions we've included in our interviews. It should open up a fascinating discussion, and we think you'll get *valuable* information that can help you better manage and motivate. You may also wish to ponder the questions we've asked the managers; you might discover some things about yourself that would be helpful in sharpening your leadership skills.

Here are our two interview formats:

INTERVIEW QUESTIONS FOR TWENTYSOMETHING WORKERS

1. What other kinds of work have you done?
2. Do you think your beliefs, attitudes, values, and philosophy of life are the same as or different than your parents'?
3. What is your most important priority—the thing that means the most to you?
4. Do you think your parents' generation were workaholics?
5. How do you want your life to be different from theirs?
6. Would you be a different kind of parent than they were?
7. If you could have the perfect job, what would it be like?
8. How about the perfect boss?
9. What keeps your current job from being ideal?
10. Do you feel you have the right skills for your job?
11. What do you think is the very best thing about your generation? The worst?

INTERVIEW QUESTIONS FOR MANAGERS

1. Are young workers today different from previous generations? How?
2. Do young workers seem to have a different work ethic than you did at their age?
3. Do you think young workers have the necessary skills to do the work?
4. Do you think young workers have different attitudes and beliefs than you?
5. What is your most difficult challenge in supervising young workers?
6. Do young workers offer any unique assets to the organization?
7. If you could change just one thing about young workers, what would it be?
8. Can you think of a time when an approach you've taken with a young worker has been less than effective?
9. What kinds of training do you think could benefit your young workers? What is your organization providing?
10. What are you or your organization doing that is helpful in managing young workers?

CHAPTER-AT-A-GLANCE

• Common themes among the three twentysomething workers:

Our parents and their generation were workaholics.
We'll be home more for our kids.
We like bosses who give us autonomy; we don't like "checkers" (bosses who constantly check up on us).

• Common themes among the three managers:

Young workers need better oral and written communication skills.
They work to live rather than live to work.
They're impatient.
They're less loyal.
They are focused on themselves.
They are enthusiastic, creative, and energetic.
We need to listen to them.

7

How to Resist an Overwhelming Urge to Choke the Living Daylights Out of Some Young Hotshot Who Desperately Needs It

Our previous chapters have worked on defining twentysomething workers. We've explored, in detail, what makes them tick and what they want, who they are and how they got to be that way. Now we shift our focus to you, the manager, and to helping you deal with the members of this generation you employ and supervise.

Many managers we've talked with express great frustration; many are ready to throw up their hands and cry "Uncle!" Many find themselves directing their energies into wishing these workers were different. Many, as we note somewhat facetiously in our title, are dangerously close to "choking the living daylights" out of some young worker.

Before wringing a vulnerable young neck, please read this chapter. We'll discuss the turbulent times and organizational shifts partially responsible for the frustration, as well as the natural generational conflicts that arise in the workplace. You will get some information on how these different generations view one another as managers and employees, and you will read about some new leadership strategies. You will hear what some companies are doing to ease the frustration level and increase mutual respect. Finally, you will learn some steps you can take now to avoid choking a valuable resource.

The Value ($) of Your Young Worker

Your young worker is immensely valuable to you—literally. Talking strictly dollars and cents, you can't afford to choke—much less lose—this precious commodity. Certainly, every young worker's value goes up as the labor pool shrinks and it becomes increasingly difficult to attract qualified entry-level employees. But perhaps even more critical is the amount of money you invest in each new employee. The cost to attract, hire, train, and benefit each fresh face in your organization ranges from $18,000 to $32,000. This is a sizable investment—one you lose if you lose your employee and have to begin the expensive cycle all over again.

Here's another way to look at it:

1. Take the hourly wage of your young worker.
2. Multiply it by 2,050 hours (a normal work period for one year).
3. Multiply this total by a factor of 2.5, which represents the employee's proportionate share of the cost of space, heat, light, furniture, equipment, etc.
4. This new total represents the actual value of your employee—far more than just a salary.

Clearly, the more prudent economic choice is to hang onto all but the very worst of your frustrating young employees, learn to accept their differences, and direct your leadership energies into helping them become productive in your organization.

How Are You Responding to Your Young Worker?

Before we move on, take a moment to evaluate your own response to your young workers by answering these true/false statements:

1. I occasionally lose patience with my young worker.
2. I find myself becoming angry with my young worker.
3. I spend a lot of time discussing my frustration level with my peers.
4. I often perform tasks myself rather than delegating them to my young worker.
5. I question the expertise of my young worker.
6. I question the loyalty of my young worker.
7. I question the dependability of my young worker.
8. I don't know how to motivate my young worker.

If you answered true more often than false, you've got lots of company. You are certainly representative of many managers we've talked with across the country. Don't be discouraged—read on!

When Generations Collide

One reason for all the frustration is simply the differences that exist between generations. These differences are played out in all areas of our lives, including the workplace, with results that range from the ordinary to the highly dramatic.

Frame of Reference

People navigate the world using their own frames of reference. A metaphor we like to use to explain this concept is that of a stained-glass window. Picture yourself at birth receiving an empty frame and beginning to construct a complex stained-glass window through which you view the world. As your awareness of the world around you grows and your interactions with others increase, you find that pieces of glass are shaped and fitted in by family, friends, teachers; all the people you connect with, your "significant others." Eventually, around the age of seven or so, your window has many of its most important pieces set, forming your unique viewpoint—the pattern of attitudes, beliefs, values, desires, and expectations you bring to all interactions.

Your frame of reference cannot help but result in interpersonal conflict; it differs from the frames of members representing different generations. Although you can't avoid such conflicts, and shouldn't, with some understanding you can certainly ease their impact. This is especially true in the workplace where three distinct generational frames—traditional, baby boomer, and younger worker—are currently caught in a traffic jam. To avoid the scratches and dents when generations collide, it is helpful to know what one generation does that drives folks from other generations nuts.

What They Do That Drives These Folks Crazy

Traditionalists
    Drive Younger Workers nuts by:
        Saying, "But we've *always* done it this way."
    Drive Baby Boomers nuts by:
        Quoting from the policy manual.

Baby Boomers
    Drive Younger Workers nuts by:
        Droning on about the "way it was" in the sixties.
    Drive Traditionalists nuts by:
        Talking to them about intimate details of their personal lives.

Younger Workers
    Drive Baby Boomers nuts by:
        Asking, "What's in it for me?"
    Drive Traditionalists nuts by:
        Breaking the rules.

Our frame of reference is greatly influenced by the generation we're a part of, and we tend to make generalizations about other generations based upon that frame.

How They View Each Other

Traditionalists See
  Baby Boomers as:
    disrespectful
    overly blunt
    too "warm and fuzzy"
  Younger Workers as:
    very young
    impatient
    unethical

Baby Boomers See
  Traditionalists as:
    caught in the by-the-book syndrome
    overly cautious, conservative
    inflexible
  Younger Workers as:
    selfish
    manipulative
    aloof

Younger Workers See
  Traditionalists as:
    old, outdated
    rigid
    obsequious
  Baby Boomers as:
    workaholic
    unrealistic
    disgustingly "new age"

Frames of Reference and Leadership Styles

Now let's take a look at baby boomers as managers, and compare them to their World War II counterparts, to help complete the chart of contrasting values. Baby-boomer managers tend to have very strong beliefs about how people should be led. Coming out of their sixties frame of reference, they believe:

- all workers should be treated humanely.
- the workplace should be friendly and warm.
- there should be equality of opinion.
- interaction between people should be consensual and participatory.

They are, above all, good team players, believing everyone wins on a winning team. As might be expected, baby-boomer managers don't always act with these noble ideals in mind. Instead, they often revert to behavior that reflects the way they themselves were first managed, much the way many of us parents unconsciously revert to the parenting style we grew up with.

Baby boomers were most likely first managed by Traditionalists, members of the World War II generation, who have an even different slant on leadership. These managers tend to:

- follow rules and procedures closely, with a "by the book" attitude.
- adhere to a traditional chain of command.
- reward loyalty and dependability.

The traditionalists' reliance on organizational structure can sometimes by interpreted as a lack of flexibility. Regarding communication and contact among workers, they prefer to follow the relay or chain-of-command process, whereby they arrange and facilitate contact on a formal basis, instead of encouraging workers to initiate direct communication themselves.

Clearly, these two styles of leadership are different, and bring with them their own positive and negative results. But what we've discovered is that, regardless of who does the managing, younger workers have clear, definite, strong feelings about how they ought to be managed. Take a look at this laundry list of what turns them on and off:

TWENTYSOMETHING WORKERS

Turn-ons	*Turn-offs*
• Recognition	• Hearing about the past (yours)
• Praise	• Inflexibility about time
• Time with you (manager)	• Workaholism
• Learning how what they're doing right now is making them more marketable	• Being watched and scrutinized
• Opportunity to learn new things	• Feeling disrespected
• Fun at work (structured play, harmless practical jokes, cartoons, light competition, surprises)	• Feeling pressure to "convert" to traditionalist behavior
• Small, unexpected rewards for jobs well done	• Disparaging comments about their generation's tastes and styles

Career Development

Along with understanding the dynamics behind the colliding generations, it is helpful to remember that we all pass through certain phases in our careers. There's always a certain amount of complaining that "kids just aren't the same today," and it's important to remember that the way we perform and interact on the job today has probably shifted considerably since our early working years. The following phases, recognized by Claire Raines and a colleague, Larry Neifert, are useful for summarizing an individual's career path:

Seven Phases of Career Development*
People typically advance through seven phases in their careers. On the average, each phase lasts about seven years. Probably, no one goes through every phase in exactly this order. Some people advance to a certain phase and remain there. Others skip a phase or two.

1. Dues-Paying.

In this first phase, most of us take on full-time or part-time jobs that are less than what we see as our true professions.

Examples: A woman with a college degree in education works as a secretary; a high school graduate who plans to become a business-man works at night as a waiter and in the day as a meter reader.

In this phase, the primary goals are gaining security and establishing ourselves in the work world.

2. Mainstreaming.

In this phase, we move into a job in our chosen profession. We are living out a dream—sometimes our parents', sometimes our own.

3. Excelling.

Approximately fourteen years after we have entered the work-force, we are doing our "life's work," and we move into a set of years marked by a sense of proficiency and confidence.

Typically, this phase ends with disillusionment. There is often a sense that we have accomplished our goals—and that, perhaps, they were not as important as we once thought. A typical feeling as this phase ends is, "Some sixteen-year-old kid decided *I* was going to be a dentist. Now, here it is twenty years later, and I've realized I *hate* being a dentist."

The end of this phase is often triggered by a "cataclysmic event"—

*Reprinted by permission. ©1991 Claire Raines and Larry Neifert.

mid-life crisis, divorce, empty nest, death in the family, or career disappointment.

4. Reassessing.

What follows is a rebirth of sorts. We move into an experimental period. We switch gears. Many people pursue "the road not taken": they go back to school for their MBA's; they start their own businesses; they make lateral moves in their corporations. Many explore completely different types of work.

This phase is marked by a willingness to explore and take risks.

5. Integrating.

Sometimes in a new niche, sometimes with a new twist on the same job, we have a new focus. Our primary task in this career phase is toward "wholism," integrating the various aspects of our lives into a unified whole.

6. Peaking.

This phase is marked by a sense of comfort and contentment with ourselves and our work.

7. Transitioning.

This phase acts as a bridge, taking us from the earlier phases into our future—whether that future holds retirement, part-time work, or another career. It offers time for review and reflection, and calls for decisions about what comes next.

A significant number of people choose not to move into this seventh phase, continuing instead the sixth phase of job comfort and contentment. Neglecting the seventh phase can be dangerous if company policy, health, or other circumstances force them into retirement.

Here's what this information has to say about your relationship with your younger worker:

- Remember that the two of you are in different phases of your careers. The way you view your job is probably very different than the way he sees his. In all honesty, many of us—outstanding as we are!—weren't all *that* fabulous at our first jobs.

- Today, with the birth dearth and resulting labor shortage, some young workers are simply skipping phase one, Dues-Paying. A few also skip phase two, Mainstreaming. A friend of ours has a brother in his twenties who is an exceptionally bright, driven, highly successful corporate attorney who, within seven years of entering the labor force, is clearly in phase three, Excelling—and earning in the triple digits.

Turbulent Times: New Leadership Strategies

Peter Drucker, guru of modern American management, labeled the nineties "turbulent times." Not a surprising assessment, unless you consider the fact that he made this prophetic statement in 1980, nearly ten years before recent dramatic events in Eastern Europe, China, and the Persian Gulf.

Drucker was uncannily accurate in predicting that American business is not immune to paradigm shifts, which we discussed in an earlier chapter. These shifts affect all areas of our day-to-day lives, such as how we communicate and how we do our work. The point we want to make here is that the reshaping of American business, coupled with global events, the shrinking labor pool, and the costs of retaining employees, makes it mandatory for supervisors to learn some new leadership strategies. Before we delve into some of them, it may be helpful to look at one important paradigm shift—the way young workers see the organization chart versus the way you, the manager, may see it.

The Organization Chart: What Professors Are Telling Them

You might be somewhat surprised by what college kids are learning in Business 101. The hierarchical organizational chart—the standard pyramid—is called the old model. It's presented as outdated. Students are told that this model was based on the industrial-age organization in which employees were regarded as the main source of physical power. Management acted as the brain; the labor force the brawn. In this type of organization, supervisors gave orders and workers did what they were told.

Traditional Pyramid

Executives
Senior Management
Middle Management
Professional Staff
Front-Line Supervisors
Front-Line Workers
Support Staff

Underlying Management Philosophy

• All people are not equal.

• Laborers are not as intelligent as management.

• Laborers can't make good decisions.

• Laborers aren't an integral part of the organization.[1]

In addition to the traditional pyramid, college students are learning two more modern models:

Inverted Pyramid

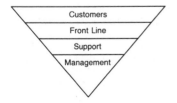

Customers
Front Line
Support
Management

Underlying Management Philosophy

• Front-line people who contact the customer are at the top.

• Support personnel who back the front-line are next.

• The role of management is to remove obstacles from the paths of workers so they can put the customer first.

• Managers and employees are trusted and empowered.

This organizational model inverts the traditional pyramid..Instead of traditional rank-and-power-based relationships, the organization empowers the front-line employee and his or her managers with authority and power to make decisions. The basic message in this model is, "You are authorized to think!"

Flattened Pyramid

Underlying Management Philosophy

- Fewer layers in the organization improve communication flow.

- In some cases, front-line and middle managers work alongside staff.

- Simplified reporting relationships improve decision-making.

This model indicates the flattening of the typical organization. Businesses today are "delayering"—removing levels of management. In the 1980s, half the *Fortune* 1,000 companies eliminated at least one layer of management. Chrysler and General Motors cut out three layers; Ford got rid of five.

Both the inverted and flattened pyramids are examples of paradigm shifts—major changes that occur when existing methods and models no longer serve as effectively as they once did. Both are based upon strong values for involvement in the workplace. The philosophy that underlies them says:

- People are equal.
- Everyone has a right to participate in decisions and processes that influence their lives.
- Employees have the ability to make good decisions.[2]

The Reality

Job attitudes have changed. Today's workers are much less accepting of authority than their predecessors. According to a recent Harris Survey, confidence in business leaders has plummeted from 55 percent in 1966 to a low 17 percent today. Workers are less loyal to their companies: they change jobs on the average of once every three-and-one-half years. Today's rebellious, irreverent, and disloyal young people have produced a demanding workforce—one which expects far more from an employer than any previous generation.

Of course, you know most businesses, government agencies, schools, and other organizations in the United States today operate by the hierarchical model. So do we; that's the reality we see as consultants working in a variety of sizes and types of companies. But, as a manager of twentysomething workers, it's important for you to know your young workers see things differently. They arrive in the workplace with a clear set of expectations—and what they expect is an organization where their opinion counts and they make a difference.

The Challenge

As leaders, it's time for all of us to make the shift if we haven't already done so. We have arrived: the industrial age has ended; the information age and its service economy are well underway. Those who have been dictators, even benevolent ones, must be willing to give up their "my way or the highway" management styles. The successful leader in the twenty-first century will be a coach, a mentor, a supporter, and a people person.

The New Supervisor

One of the first realizations today's new supervisors are going to have to make is that often they will be expected to supervise work they don't personally know, understand, or have the training to perform. This is a direct result of the flatter organizational chart in which middle management is downsized and eliminated. Whereas supervisors once served as a relay point, they are now being expected to do what those directly beneath them do. They must not only supervise the people performing the work, but the actual work itself. The difficulty arises in assuming multiple roles: managing process, policy, and procedure; and leading people at the same time.

The Shift to Coaching

Another paradigm shift as we move from a manufacturing to a service economy is that managers must make the adjustment away from a directing leadership style to a coaching, or enabling, one. Today's effective supervisor must constantly help remove any obstacles that prevent his or her employees from achieving their goals. If we were to describe the directing style in one sentence, it might be "Here's what needs to be done—now do it!" The more effective, coaching style would sound more like "Here's what needs to be done. How can I help you to do it?"

The Platinum Rule

Here's another confusing change. Instead of the Golden Rule we grew up with, "Do unto others as you would have them do unto you," we should wisely adjust to what we call the Platinum Rule. It says, "Do unto others as they wish to be done unto." The Golden Rule, applied generically, is great. But when dealing with those who are *different* than we are, it's wiser to keep those differences in mind and act accordingly. In other words, know what buttons to push. As humorist G. K. Chesterton once said, "Do *not* do unto others as you would have them do unto you—their taste may be different!"

Enrollment vs. Empowerment

Finally, the new supervisor must be prepared to empower employees, in an attempt to keep them productive and challenged. It's been said you can't actually empower others, but that you can enroll them in a cause, which can result in empowerment. Robert White is chairman and chief executive of ARC International, a firm that works with companies making major changes. White says, "In the old style that U.S. business has been operating under, work is about getting things done. The old model has rules, goals, structures. In the future, a new model has to be used. The grounding point has to be why we are here. If you don't bring everyone into the equation and connect with the vision of what you want to accomplish, you become color-blind. There has to be a movement in business from controlling people to empowering them."[3]

Helping the Younger Worker Learn the Ropes

As we move from the theoretical realm to the practical world of attracting, hiring, training, and developing these young workers, we recommend you do two things: help them learn the ropes and create a culture for them in your workplace.

Helping young workers learn the ropes is a process which begins in the attracting/hiring phase. When you are interviewing and eventually orienting the new employee, be sure you are clearly communicating exactly what the job will be so that young new employees aren't overly idealistic about what the work entails. Many a young worker has gone from a rather glamorous college internship into a "real" job only to discover that it is routine, dull, and even boring.

Show your new workers specifically how what they will be doing now can benefit them in the future—relate the work to an eventual goal. Help them understand the power structure of your organization, how policy is set, how decisions are made. Give them that forbidden glimpse into the inner workings of your company, and let them know that change may be slow to happen. Finally, on the most basic level, don't assume they know how to dress, where the bathrooms are, how long they should take for breaks and lunch. Information is power, and an empowered employee reduces your frustration.

When you create a work culture for your young employees, you help them feel a part of something bigger than themselves and motivate them to make a contribution. Again, this can happen during the orientation phase, when you share the legends and lore of the workplace. Tell them the "story" of the company in a social setting, complete with history and legends. Are there people to emulate? Shared anecdotes that lend a feeling of humanity and even levity to the workplace? All of these things, though simple in nature, have a substantial impact on the future success of your young worker.

What Two Companies Are Doing

Many of the managers we've spoken to have offered their unique solutions to the problems facing them in supervising young workers. Their ideas range from the ordinary and logical to the outlandishly creative. We thought you might like knowing what these two highly visible and successful companies are doing.

Ben & Jerry's

With over $77 million in ice cream sales by 1990, and a workforce that doubled in 1988, cofounders Ben Cohen and Jerry Greenfield are understandably devoted to keeping their employees satisfied and loyal. These two ice cream entrepreneurs, whose product is sold in forty-six states, have been described as "the ultimate benign bosses in the friendliest of employee-friendly firms," and the "archetype of a growing corporate culture of caring, where workers expect more from their jobs than just a paycheck."[4]

Worker after worker describes being at Ben & Jerry's in absolutely glowing terms. "It's what a job should be," says one. "It's not just making money, but doing good things."[5] Another worker, in her mid-thirties, vows she'll stay at her job until retirement.

Their secret? Check out this list of available benefits:

- free health club benefits
- profit sharing
- college tuition
- 7.5 percent of the company's pretax profits dished out to worthy social causes selected by employees

A day-care center opened in 1990. A typical day for a worker may include "choosing which production task she'll [the worker] do. Every day she runs the risk of getting a free backrub or having a hilarious run-in with the company's Joy Gang."[6]

Then there's one final benefit, the icing on the cake, you might say. Each of Ben & Jerry's 400 employees have the daily option of taking home three free pints of ice cream!

McDonald's

Not surprisingly, almost half of all people working for McDonald's Corporation are under the age of twenty. That makes it the largest corporate employer of youth in the United States. These 240,000 young people from across the nation represent an enormous management challenge, and McDonald's is rising to the task. Far from simply offering low-paying, dead-end jobs flipping burgers, McDonald's teaches kids "the discipline and skills they need for a productive future—particularly to minorities and low-income employees, who may lack a structured home life."[7]

Some of the incentives offered to young workers are quick advancement, such as the fast track to crew chief made by one seventeen-year-old in just a few months of employment. Also, "McDonald's has a long tradition of promoting on the basis of skill and hustle, not academic credentials. More than half of its corporate executives never graduate from college."[8]

You've probably seen the McDonald's television ads featuring senior citizens and developmentally challenged adults who sing the praises of working for McDonald's, where putting on the uniform and successfully performing their tasks gives them a feeling of pride and a sense of family.

While they don't provide many special training or educational programs, McDonald's concentrates on teaching kids *how* to work—knowledge that can contribute to a brighter future. Says the seventeen-year-old Harlem resident we mentioned before, "Where else can I go at my age and be over this many people?"[9]

TAKING ACTION

This chapter is full of steps you can take now to become a more effective leader of the twentysomething generation. Here are two further action items: using benefits and contracts.

When your communications include benefits—that is, when they answer the question "What's in it for me?"—you increase the chances of getting the results you want from your twentysomething employees. The following exercise helps you develop your skill in giving directives to young workers.

What's in It for Me?
For each of these tasks, write a directive that includes at least one benefit. Number 1 shows you what we mean.

1. *Task:* filing.

Filing these papers will help you get an overview of this project and how it fits into our business.

2. *Task:* putting away tools.

_____

_____

3. *Task:* typing a letter.

_____

_____

4. *Task:* making a phone call.

_____

_____

5. *Task:* attending a meeting.

_____

_____

6. *Task:* getting to work on time.

_____

_____

Develop a Contract with Your Younger Worker
The contract is another important tool at your disposal for easing the frustration that comes when expectations are not met. Twentysomethings have operated with contracts before—their teachers and busy parents used "if . . . then" styles. A great example of a baby boomer designing a contract on-the-fly is in the movie *Three Men and a Baby.* Tom Selleck portrays an affluent architect. In a favorite scene, a roommate catches him as he rushes out the door, late to meet a client, saying, "The baby just did a diddle, and it's your turn to change her diapers." Selleck responds, "I'll give you a thousand dollars if you'll do it." This is the type of contract the twentysomething generation has grown used to.

The contract is an agreement between you and your young worker about a task or work goal. Though the contract doesn't have to be formally written, we recommend you consider the following suggestions as the two of you meet about a project:

In the Contract

Is there agreement about:

1. the task to be accomplished or goal to be achieved?
2. the completion date?
3. the dates for check-in about progress?
4. the standards of results expected?

5. availability and use of resources?
6. how success will be evaluated or measured?
7. what happens if something goes wrong?
8. reward and recognition?

An excellent resource for constructing contracts with employees is *Personal Performance Contracts* by Roger Fritz.[10]

Notes

1. Ken Adams and Claire Raines, *The Big Chill Generation at Work,* unpublished manuscript, 1987.
2. Ibid.
3. *Colorado Business,* December 1990, p. 36.
4. Carol Clurmar, "More Than Just a Paycheck," *USA Weekend,* January 19, 1990, pp. 4–5.
5. Ibid.
6. Ibid.
7. Marcus Mabry, "Inside the Golden Arches," *Newsweek,* December 18, 1989, p. 45.
8. Ibid.
9. Ibid.
10. Crisp Publications, Inc. books may be ordered from Bradford, Inc., 129 W. 10th Ave., Denver, CO 80204, (303) 892-0544.

CHAPTER-AT-A-GLANCE

- The value of young workers goes up as the labor pool shrinks and it becomes increasingly difficult to attract qualified entry-level employees.

- We each navigate the world through our own frame of reference, our complex "stained glass window" through which we view the world. Each frame of reference is different and particular to our childhood and influence of parents, teachers, and friends, and the world as it was when we were growing up.

- Because of our different frames, we cannot help but have interpersonal conflicts with the other generations. Although these conflicts are unavoidable, understanding how traditionalists, baby boomers, and young workers view one another can ease the impact.

- Twentysomething workers have certain management behaviors across the board that definitely turn them on, such as recognition and praise, and turn them off, such as being watched and scrutinized.

- We all pass through career phases, and the way we perform as established workers and managers probably has shifted considerably during our working years.

- The seven phases of career development are dues-paying, mainstreaming, excelling, reassessing, integrating, peaking, and transitioning.

- Managers and supervisors must learn new leadership strategies in leading twentysomething workers.

- Young workers are learning a new management model in business classes that gives more power to front-line employees and flattens the organizational chart.

- The successful leader of the twenty-first century will be a coach, a mentor, a supporter, and a people person.

- Today's workers are less loyal to their companies, change jobs on the average of once every three-and-one-half years, are rebellious and irreverent, and expect more from an employer than any previous generation.

- Today's workers want an organization where their opinions count and where they can make a difference.

8

Flexi-Leadership: A New Skill for the 1990s

As a business leader moving into the twenty-first century, the only thing you can count on is *change*—changing economics, changing markets, changing strategies, and most important, a changing workforce. The demands on you are tremendous. As we see it, your success at meeting those demands will be determined by one skill above all others: your ability to be flexible. How *adaptable* you are to shifting conditions, how *responsive* you are to the people around you, how willing you are to *bend* to meet the situation: these capabilities will be the keys to your success.

In this chapter, we explore the four critical attributes of the Workforce 2000 leaders. Then, instead of us simply *telling* you about flexibility, you will have the opportunity to test your own skills. You will get acquainted with six young people working in different parts of the country in a variety of industries. We'll ask you how you would adapt your leadership style for each situation and worker. Finally, we'll recommend a leadership approach for each of the six based on the values systems you read about in chapter three.

By the way, you may have noticed our tendency to talk about leadership rather than management. Today's young people want to be led—not managed. "You can *lead* your horse to water, but you can't *manage* him to drink."[2] People are going to continue to manage themselves. They'll do *what* they want, *when* they want, the *way* they want—based on their desires, their values, and their own personal situations. We can't change people. We can only change ourselves. We can lead others—and it's time we got started.

The Workforce 2000 Leader

The twentysomething workforce—with the unique set of problems and promises we've outlined in our previous chapters—demands a new type of leader. Many of the "brash pack" refuse to put up with hard-line authority. Those who have taken business courses arrive on the job expecting participative leadership. Those with poor basic skills cannot be expected to make it on their own. Many aren't motivated by your company's existing incentives. Their demand for flextime, along with their notion that work should be fun, may stretch your policies to the breaking point. The new workforce is challenging our processes to the max! How will you manage?

The successful leader will operate from these four key leadership principles:

1. I can only lead someone I know.
A few years ago, American business operated under the assumption that employees left their personal baggage at the front door. Today we know workers bring their lives with them through the door and onto the job. When war broke out in the Persian Gulf, ARC International, a training and consulting firm, held sessions about the war and its effects on employees. Some were concerned about relatives or friends in the Gulf. Virtually all had the war on their minds.

Thinking, feeling, young adult workers are complicated creatures—whole human beings with lives and problems and issues that deeply affect the way they do business. Leaders who spend time with their people, who *listen,* and who understand the complexities of their employees' lives have the necessary information to truly lead.

125

2. I am a coach.
The new workforce demands a coach, a supporter, and a people-person who challenges workers to reach their potential. Workers who feel listened to and acknowledged are much more likely to be productive than those who feel that the boss doesn't give a damn. With high technology and the information age expanding industry's knowledge base at breakneck speed, more and more leaders are finding they may not know how to *do* the work their people are doing; what they *can do* is challenge, nurture, and coach in ways that increase productivity and expand their workers' knowledge base.

3. I value people.
In a manufacturing economy, production, equipment, and systems determined the company's success. In today's economy, those who are succeeding in quality, cost, and service are those who take full advantage of the workforce's potential. As Tom Peters says in his chapter on leadership in *Thriving on Chaos,* "People *must* become the primary source of value added."[3]

4. I involve people.
We've already noted the trend in *Fortune* 500 companies over the past five years to get rid of layers of management. As this trend continues, there is a growing need for the frontline worker—the one who meets with the customer, deals with the vendor, or operates the machinery—to take on roles previously ascribed to managers. The most important of these roles, accountability, rarely takes place unless the employee contributes to goal-setting, takes part in policy-making, acts as part of the evaluation process, and feels like a valuable member of the team. Says Peters, "There is no limit to what the average person can accomplish if thoroughly involved."[4]

Flexibility

Leaders who act on these four values—leading by knowing, coaching, valuing, and involving people—will garner information that will then test their personal flexibility. What they learn by truly getting to know their people, by listening, and by receiving their input, will give them information that demands change. As Max DePree explains in his extraordinary book, *Leadership Is an Art,* "we cannot become what we need to be by remaining what we are."[5] So effective leaders of the twentysomething generation will be those who are not only willing to change the status quo around them but who themselves are willing to grow and change.

Six Young Workers

Here are descriptions of six uniquely different twentysomething workers. Each has his or her own set of values; all live in different parts of the country; every one works in a different industry; their work performance varies widely. Your challenge, as you read this section, will be to explore the flexibility of your own leadership style. As you read about each young worker, ask yourself, "How would I lead this person in such a way that I would retain, challenge, and develop him or her, while maximizing productivity?" We'll give you an assortment of leadership options to choose from at the end of the descriptions. Then we'll give you our recommendations on a leadership style tailored to each worker.

Beth

Beth, twenty-six, works in retail sales for a well-known computer manufacturer in the Silicon Valley. For the last two years, she has won awards for exceeding corporate sales goals for her division. The daughter of two university professors, Beth grew up in Palo Alto, California, and finished her MBA when she was twenty-two. A confident, well-spoken young woman, Beth talks so fast it is often difficult to keep up with her. She dresses impeccably in expensive suits and silk shirts, and drives a new sports car. A private person, Beth is efficient, organized, and pleasant, although she has few close relationships at work. Her supervisor has had difficulty warming up to her and knows very little about her personal life.

In many ways, Beth seems like an ideal employee: she is self-motivated, intelligent, and productive. Her supervisor came to us, however, with three major concerns. First, he worried that Beth had nearly "topped out"—after only four years, she was earning more than many people will earn at the peak of their careers; she had won all the sales awards the company offers; and she had reached the top of her career path. Another concern emerged in a recent regional sales conference. The previous year, the regional director had set up a competition between divisions aimed at increasing sales of a new product. Due to a questionable interpretation of the original goals, Beth's group was passed over for the award. She acted childish when she expressed her anger and frustration over losing the award. As a result, her supervisor received a stern warning from the regional director about handling employees effectively. The other issue Beth's supervisor worries about is her relationship with others in the office. She is not well liked by the administrative staff or the other sales people; indeed, she is the source of many complaints. Beth's coworkers accuse her of being self-focused and insensitive. They complain she takes advantage of them and takes them for granted.

Alberto
Alberto, twenty-seven, works for the director of management development in the corporate headquarters of a national insurance company based in Omaha, Nebraska. The director hired Alberto four years ago as a "go-fer" to set up training rooms, copy and collate seminar materials, set up audiovisual equipment, and run errands. Alberto quickly proved to be an outstanding worker: he is dependable, stable, and loyal. Al consistently follows through on every assignment he is given, and his supervisor knows this is a worker

she can always count on. A sensitive, concerned leader herself, she has expanded his responsibilities with every personnel review. He now videotapes many of the company's meetings and seminars and works as a liaison between the training department and its outside consultants. Al's quiet, easy manner and personal vitality have earned him a reputation throughout the seventeen-story building. Everyone knows Alberto.

Al finished high school and then joined the Marine Corps, where he says he learned "to be respectful, to do what I'm told, and to do it right the first time." After his discharge from the Marines, he returned to Omaha, his hometown, where he married his high school sweetheart. The marriage lasted only eighteen months, but produced a son, whom Alberto sees on weekends and holidays. Today, a hefty monthly child-support payment takes a big chunk out of Alberto's small salary.

Here's another employee who may sound ideal, yet his supervisor is doing the right thing to spend some time brainstorming about his career. Although he is a promising young man, without further education Alberto will reach a dead end. His basic skills are just that—*basic*. He needs improvement in reading, writing, and math if he is going to take on other responsibilities. His salary is dictated by the corporate structure—based on responsibilities, education, and experience—and it is barely enough for him to live on. Unlike many of his twentysomething counterparts, Al is absolutely loyal to his manager and company. He loves his job. Yet the strength of his loyalty may actually prove to be a problem in terms of his career advancement. Unless he takes on some new challenges and makes some personal changes, he may stagnate and become a long-term, burned-out employee stuck in the bureaucracy.

Charmaine

After finishing a two-year community college program in administrative skills, Charmaine, twenty-three, worked five secretarial jobs before coming to the federal agency in Washington, D.C., where she is now employed. Charmaine grew up in Washington, the child of loving and liberal parents who have been deeply involved in national politics for many years. She is a nice young woman who received good recommendations from all her previous employers. Charmaine has great people skills: she is a good listener, is very sensitive to those around her, and is a great team player.

If Charmaine were to leave this job, her current supervisor would probably feel compelled to write the same "good" recommendation he got from all her previous employers. Yet the hard, cold truth about Charmaine is: she's a barely mediocre performer. It appears she simply doesn't want to work too hard. If she is motivated by something, her employers have yet to discover what it is. In a recent interview with her supervisor, he complained that Charmaine brings an array of personal problems, primarily revolving around her boyfriend, to work. Secretaries and coworkers from her office and the one across the hall have a hard time getting their work done because of Charmaine's lengthy updates about the circumstances of her personal life. She has developed a close friendship with her supervisor and relishes time alone with him. But he, too, has heard far more than he cares to about Charmaine's life outside of work.

Rosa

Rosa, nineteen, is a waitress in a large upscale delicatessen and restaurant in Miami. The restaurant is located in the heart of a trendy financial district populated by young, wealthy businesspeople. It is only a few blocks from where Rosa lives with her large extended family. Her parents immigrated to the United States just a year ago. Cousins and other relatives continue to arrive; some are clearly working illegally in this country. Two of Rosa's brothers work at the restaurant: one is a busboy, the other a dishwasher. Rosa is willing to work double shifts and overtime to keep her family afloat.

Her work performance has its ups and downs. Although her English skills are not advanced and she speaks her native language with other Spanish-speaking coworkers, she does what she needs to to get by. Rosa tries hard to please, and the customers like her. She is not assertive with them, though, when she needs to be. She seems to lack understanding of some of the busy restaurant's policies—about special orders, for example. Thus she often gets caught between the cook and her customers when the cook refuses to prepare special orders she has promised. Her most prevalent work-related problem is tardiness: it seems she is late nearly as often as she is on time. Rosa's family responsibilities are so great they sometimes pull her in two different directions. Once, when it was time to be at work, she was delayed because she had to take her grandmother to the doctor. Another time she was late because no one else was at home to care for an infant.

Bobby
Bobby, twenty-seven, is a lineman with a utilities company in rural Georgia. Growing up poor in a family with six children and an abusive father, Bobby learned early to fend for himself. Today, he comes across as a tough guy; his protective shell is virtually impenetrable. Cynical and sarcastic when approached, he is distrustful and rarely speaks to his "bossman" unless spoken to first. Bobby was hired right out of high school when he was seventeen and has never had another job.

A quick review of his personnel record reveals that Bobby is actually a decent worker, especially when he works alone. In his ten-year history with the company, there have been a few complaints from customers and coworkers about his abrasiveness, but his performance in general has been satisfactory. However, things have gotten difficult lately where Bobby is concerned. The company is going through a major cultural shift—working to move accountability, leadership, and decision-making down to the front-line worker. Most of the employees are fairly skeptical about these changes, particularly since 7 percent of their fellow workers were laid off three months ago. But Bobby is more than skeptical; he distrusts all managers and is certain "things will never change."

Frankly, he's not sure he wants them to. A loner by nature, he is now being asked to attend meetings, express his opinions in front of large groups of people, and become an active visionary in the "new culture." For Bobby, the final straw was getting notice that he would be expected to attend a three-day personal effectiveness seminar that would help him learn how he could become involved and make an active contribution to the "new" company.

Paul

Paul is a nineteen-year-old college student who has taken the winter off to work as a lift operator at a Utah ski resort. In his high school years, Paul, an exceptional student who relished the hard courses like chemistry and physics, was labeled a "nerd." A whiz on the computer, he is fascinated by technology and how things work. When there are occasional mechanical problems with the ski lifts, he is a strong asset. Paul is passionate about skiing. Spending the winter in Utah was his idea of heaven-on-earth.

Supervising Paul, however, is less than heavenly. He questions and wants to discuss at length every assignment he's given—along with every policy and procedure by which the ski area operates. Impatient with his fellow lift operators, Paul is definitely not a team player. He seems to hold management in low esteem; his supervisor senses that Paul has judged him to be less than brilliant. Paul complains the job isn't as much fun as he expected, and he is easily bored with the routine nature of the work. When 4:00 P.M. arrives—whether there's still work to do or not—Paul is out the door and into his bindings for the last run of the day.

Flex Your Leadership Muscles

So now you've met this chapter's six twentysomething workers, and it's time to explore leadership styles adapted specifically for each of them. Before you take the inventory below, you may want to glance back over chapter three, where we examined the six major values systems from the MindMaker6™.

For each young worker profiled in this chapter and listed below, first identify that worker's primary value system. Then select the leadership style you think would work most effectively:

WORKER
Beth, 26, computer sales, Silicon Valley

Primary value system _____

Leadership style _____

Alberto, 27, odd jobs and video production, management development department, insurance industry, Omaha

Primary value system _____

Leadership style _____

Charmaine, 23, secretary, federal agency, Washington, D.C.

Primary value system _____

Leadership style _____

Rosa, 19, waitress, Miami

Primary value system _____

Leadership style _____

Bobby, 27, lineman, utilities company, rural Georgia

Primary value system _____

Leadership style _____

Paul, 19, lift operator, ski industry, Utah

Primary value system _____

Leadership style _____

Six Leadership Strategies

Based on the MindMaker6™ and what we know about the twentysomething generation, here (pages 135–136) are leadership styles we recommend for managing and motivating each of the six workers we've described.

LEADERSHIP STYLE

Style A
- Encourage this worker to get counseling through the employee assistance program.
- Make this worker part of a production team and train the group to deal with team members' performance problems as they arise.
- Use lunch with you as a reward for this worker.
- Be warm and caring.

Style B
- Allow this employee to work alone; don't force participation.
- Offer challenges to this worker.
- Deal one-on-one with this employee.
- Be assertive.

Style C
- Show how career counseling offers high return on investment.
- Encourage quick movement on the management track.
- Stress the practical payoffs of improving on-the-job relationships and people skills ("getting ahead through relationship").
- When working with this employee, move quickly; stay action-oriented.

Style D
- Offer freedom and privacy as rewards.
- Encourage this worker to be creative in ways that make the job more *fun*.

LEADERSHIP STYLE *(Continued)*

- Demonstrate how rules and policies contribute to the proper functioning of the overall system.
- Stress personal accountability.
- Show your competence.

Style E
- Offer a long-term reward for returning to school.
- Give strong guidance to help this worker find the correct academic program.
- Encourage this worker to serve on company committees and task forces.
- Be "the boss."

Style F
- Assign this worker to a supervisor from the same family or group.
- Personally assist this worker with rules and procedures until they become habit.
- Provide support and security for things like promptness and short-term anniversaries.
- Stay nearby and be supportive.

Leading Beth

Beth exemplifies *Achiever* values. She is motivated by status and material things; she values action; she is self-oriented; and she is extremely productive. Generally, Achievers are motivated by challenging goals, clearly outlined standards, rewards with status, and independence.[6] The most productive environment offers opportunities for personal advancement and high levels of involvement in the process of reaching goals.

Since Beth has nearly topped out in her current job track, there is a danger of losing her. Beth needs some career counseling to identify possible areas for advancement. By offering her new challenges, your company is more likely to retain her—and she is more likely to be satisfied. We recommend the leadership track. To succeed there, Beth clearly needs improved communication and interpersonal skills. Beth is unlikely to work on these skills without a tangible reward; that simply isn't her nature. But advancement on the leadership track offers her that reward. Getting Beth to increase her interpersonal skills will help you with all three major concerns about her performance: her need for new challenges, the regional director's reaction to her childish expression of anger, and the staff's complaints about her abrasiveness.

As an effective leader, you will need to use good sales skills with Beth. In other words, you will be most productive with her when you show her the payoffs, stress short-term results, and word your message in terms of her self-interest. The career development program you design together must be an *immediate* one. Beth and other Achievers do not succeed when they're called upon to wait and be patient. In general, we recommend you use *Leadership Style C* with Beth.

Leading Alberto
Alberto's predominant value system is *Loyalist*. His dependability, stability, consistency, and respect for leadership, along with his background in the Marines, are all clues to his primary values system. Losing Alberto as an employee is not an issue you are likely to face as Al's manager. His loyalty to you and your company will tend to keep him on board. However, without further basic skills, Alberto's job will become unsatisfying to him and you will be missing an important opportunity to develop a valuable human resource. Your challenge is to keep Alberto from joining the ranks of the hundreds of thousands of bureaucrats stuck in dead-end positions in U.S. organizations.

Because of the Loyalist's respect for leadership, your opinions are very important to Alberto. And he is likely to do what you recommend. Use your influence. Guide him into a local community-college program, where he can improve his reading, writing, math, and basic business skills. You can do everything short of actually making the decision for him. For completing a degree or certification program, offer him a reward, not necessarily monetary. It might even be an award at an employee event. The goal and the award can be long-term; Loyalists will work long and hard for delayed rewards.

Look for means other than promotion for increasing Alberto's job experience. One possibility would be to include him on company committees and task forces. This would enhance his visibility in the organization and give him opportunities to broaden his base of work experience. This experience, together with further education, will allow Alberto to grow and develop while he continues to be the great employee you know you can count on. This plan is based on *Leadership Style E.*

Leading Charmaine
Charmaine has strong *Involver* values. She views the world as a supportive, humane place. She believes in harmony and love. She is sensitive to others and has a strong need for intimacy and personal relationship. She is an excellent team player. Generally, as a leader, you will motivate Involvers by encouraging them to work in partnership with others, involving them in decision-making, and encouraging personal growth. Spending personal time—over a cup of coffee or lunch—with their bosses is seen as a reward by Involvers.

As a worker, Charmaine needs a fire lit under her to break through her barely mediocre performance record. You can successfully light that fire by forming and including Charmaine on a production team of support staff. She will thrive in a team environment, and her bond to the other team members will offer her the motivation she needs. If you see to it that the group gets good training in dealing with performance problems immediately on a peer basis, you will remove the burden of disciplining her from yourself. An added benefit will be increased communication, feedback, and assertiveness skills for the other support staff. Actually, they should not have turned to you to handle their concern about Charmaine interrupting them. They need to deal with such situations themselves. Investing time in your support staff now will save you headaches over the long haul.

Charmaine should be encouraged to get counseling about her personal issues. They are obviously interfering with the quality of her work. As long as you remain caring and supportive in the way you aim her toward counseling, she should be easily sold on the idea, since Involvers hold personal growth in high esteem. We recommend you use *Leadership Style A* with Charmaine.

Leading Rosa

Rosa displays *Kinsperson* values. The first priority in her life is the survival of her large extended family. She is willing to make personal sacrifices to provide them with income and security. As her leader, your success will depend on your ability to balance her responsibilities—to her family and to her job. If you expect her to be self-guided and motivated by traditional career success, you will fail with Rosa. Your immediate leadership goals with Rosa should be to guide her into following the restaurant's policies, which will require that she be more assertive with customers and decrease her tardiness. To accomplish these goals, it is important that you realize Rosa's work is simply a means to an end: the survival of her family.

A Kinsperson is easily intimidated by authority—particularly authority figures from outside cultures. Therefore, you will be most effective with Rosa by being helpful, supportive, soft-spoken, and protective, showing her you can be trusted. Model pleasant but assertive communications with customers for her a number of times. Or, better yet, let her learn from another employee she trusts. If one of Rosa's relatives or another member of her cultural group can be appointed her supervisor, this will increase her productivity. Demonstrate to Rosa your respect for her family, culture, and traditions, and help her to see that consistent work performance offers support and security.

We recommend you establish a small reward—monetary would be best—for a two-week term of appearing for work on time daily. Create a family feeling for Rosa at work. Remain nearby; Rosa is not a worker who thrives on working independently. As long as you are gentle, you can guide her through good work procedures until they become habit for her. This plan is based on *Leadership Style F*.

Leading Bobby

Bobby exhibits the *Loner* value system. You can recognize his values system by noting his toughness, protective shell, distrust of authority, preference for working alone, and discomfort with his company's trend to include him. You won't find lots of Loners in today's workforce, but even one can break the back of a work team. Mismanaging a Loner can lead to dire consequences. Forcing a Loner onto a team project or an interactive committee can result in a great deal of frustration for the Loner and his or her coworkers. As a leader, if you take the Loner's anger personally and try to outmaneuver him, his tenacity and stubbornness will probably get the best of you.

Allow Bobby to work alone as much as you can. Give him challenges—especially physical ones. Don't try to monitor Bobby too closely. As long as you know he's getting the job done, you'll be most effective if you "stay out of his face." Give him short-term—daily or weekly—goals and rewards. Deal with Bobby privately. Don't bring him in for a group meeting to outline a new policy or procedure. Get together with him away from others to tell him about the change. Deliver your message in a strong, assertive, tough-but-fair way. He'll respect you for it.

Rather than including Bobby in a blanket invitation to the three-day personal-effectiveness seminar, meet with him privately. Explain the purpose of the seminar and let Bobby decide how he can fulfill that purpose. An Outward Bound type of experience may accomplish the same objectives but be a better fit for Bobby's values. Or Bobby may decide to go to the seminar with the rest of your employees—but now more willingly and by his own choice.

Likewise, show Bobby you respect him. Expecting him to become a warm, caring team player is unrealistic. Instead, keep your distance and let him know you consider his unique contribution a valuable one, however it is packaged. Use *Leadership Style B* with Bobby.

Leading Paul

Choice-Seekers value efficient systems, competence, personal freedom, and privacy. Clues that Paul has Choice-Seeker values are his academic record, his fascination with computers, technology, and systems, and his impatience with routine. To keep Paul at the ski area for the rest of the season and maximize his performance, you as his leader will need to encourage him to make the work fun, protect him from the routine of policy and procedure, and make your expectations clear about the end of the work day.

The Choice-Seeker prefers to work for a technically competent leader who provides information and offers independence and privacy. Spend time up front with Paul acquainting him with the ski area operations as a system. This will give him a meaningful context in which to place all those rules and procedures. When you communicate to him about a policy, demonstrate to him how it affects the efficiency of the entire system. Don't allow yourself to be intimidated by Paul's intelligence; keep in mind your own personal strengths, and move him into the leadership role when it makes sense for the project.

If you're unwilling to let Paul ski away at the stroke of 4:00 P.M., explain the functional need for him to remain until the work is done. If he understands how he contributes to the smooth running of the system, he'll stick around. He won't stay around based on loyalty or friendship, or because it seems like the right thing to do. Finally, encourage Paul to invent his own ways of making the job *fun*. His creative mind should come up with some great ideas. We recommend *Leadership Style D* for Paul.

A Leadership Paradox

"Time out!" you may be calling. "Foul ball! My employees whine and complain if I'm not fair and consistent. One of their chief demands is for consistency in policies and procedures, the way they're enforced, and who they apply to. Now you are telling me to handle each one differently."

Yes, we know. Consistency is essential. So is individualization.

Excellence in leadership involves paradox, the marriage of contradictions. So, yes, we absolutely agree with your employees: you need to be fair in establishing, carrying out, and enforcing rules. Your workers all need to be treated humanely—with respect and dignity and concern and reverence. Yet, at the same time, all of your workers are different, today more than ever before. Mindless adherence to a consistent doctrine of discipline and management will simply not work. Only an individualized leadership style, designed especially for each worker's unique values, personality, needs, and situation capitalizes on the richness of your most valuable resource: your people. Those leaders who can remain fair while adapting their leadership style will succeed with the twentysomething workforce.

TAKING ACTION

When you understand values systems, you can individualize your approach to each worker. This list will act as a quick reference to remind you of the leadership styles generally preferred by each of the six systems from the MindMaker6™.

LEADERSHIP STYLES BASED ON WORKER VALUES*

Worker	How to Motivate This Young Worker	The Environment in Which This Worker Is Most Productive
Kinsperson	· Be protective · Spell out roles · Be helpful and supportive	· Is secure and stable · Provides a place for "togetherness" · Allows workers to produce as a group rather than individually
Loner	· Allow independence · Keep your distance · Offer opportunities for risk · Be tough and assertive · Provide short-term goals and rewards	· Doesn't force teamwork · Is physically intense
Loyalist	· Assert your authority · Spell out the rules · Reward long-term loyalty · Keep your language conservative	· Is stable · Has a clear chain of command
Achiever	· Set challenging goals · Clearly outline standards · Offer rewards with status · Encourage independence	· Is fast-paced and action-oriented · Allows opportunities for personal advancement · Offers high levels of freedom

*Adapted from MindMaker6™

LEADERSHIP STYLES BASED ON WORKER VALUES *(Continued)*

Worker	*How to Motivate This Young Worker*	*The Environment in Which This Worker Is Most Productive*
Involver	• Be a friend • Involve the employee in meetings, decisions • Spend time together	• Is cooperative and humane • Encourages personal growth • Is casual • Fosters teamwork
Choice-Seeker	• Exhibit competence • Offer independence • Provide information	• Is well-planned and efficient • Offers privacy • Has state-of-the-art equipment and systems

Notes

1. Max DePree, *Leadership Is an Art,* Doubleday, 1989, p. 30.
2. Paraphrase of a United Technologies advertisement from the *Wall Street Journal* and quoted in *SuperLeadership: Leading Others to Lead Themselves* by Charles C. Hanz and Henry P. Sims.
3. Tom Peters, *Thriving on Chaos,* Harper & Row, 1987, p. 344.
4. Ibid., p. 340.
5. DePree, p. 87.
6. Kenneth L. Adams and Dudley Lynch, MindMaker6™, Brain Technologies Corporation, 1988.

CHAPTER-AT-A-GLANCE

• As a business leader, there is one thing you can count on as you move through the nineties: change. Your success as a leader will be based on your ability to adapt, respond, and bend to the conditions around you.

• Many of the brash pack will arrive on the job expecting participative management and won't respond to hard-line authority.

• A successful leader in the twenty-first century will operate from four key principles: I can only lead someone I know, I am a coach, I value people, and I involve people.

• Leaders who act on these four principles: knowing, coaching, valuing, and involving people, will garner information that will then test their personal flexibility.

• Motivating Kinspersons: be helpful, supportive, soft spoken, and protective, showing them that you, as a manager, can be trusted.

• Motivating Loners: allow them to work alone as much as possible, provide challenges—especially physical ones—and avoid monitoring them too closely. Be assertive, tough, and fair.

• Motivating Loyalists: use your influence and respect for authority; set up long-term rewards. Rely and depend on their loyalty.

• Motivating Achievers: set challenging goals, clearly outline standards, reward with status and independence.

• Motivating Involvers: encourage them to work in partnership with others, involve them in decision-making, and encourage personal growth.

• Motivating Choice-Seekers: offer independence and privacy, encourage innovation and the fun aspects of the job.

• A successful leader today must develop an individualized leadership style, keeping in mind the unique personality, values, and motivating factors of each individual.

*The supervisor is a matador with bull coming
from both sides.*[1]

—Gene Perret

9

How to Help Young Supervisors Avoid the Yellow Sneaker Syndrome

Andrew, a twentysomething supervisor, was angry and confused. He had been promoted to his first supervisory position only four months ago at age twenty-six. His technical skills in information systems, a degree in business systems management, and his extraordinarily hard work had attracted the attention of senior management. When Mary, Andrew's supervisor, was promoted to manager, Andrew was tapped to fill her supervisor's job. He was the youngest supervisor in the company, responsible for leading a group of six information-system specialists, five of them in their thirties and one in her forties. None of them expected that Andrew would be named to replace Mary.

"I don't know what I'm doing wrong," Andrew complained to his boss, Paul. "Half the time when I explain how the new system is supposed to work, they look at me like I'm speaking gibberish. The rest of the time they just smile at me like I'm a kid or something and do whatever they want."

"You've got 'yellow sneaker syndrome,' " Paul said. "What I mean is you've lost your self-confidence. You're paying attention to the wrong things and you've peed on your own sneakers.

"I think I know how it might have happened. See, Andrew,

when you try to 'teach' them, they think you're showing off your college degree. Do you know that not one of those systems specialists has anything more than a two-year technical certificate? Also, you *are* young. Don't apologize for it. But let them know you value their years of experience and you want to learn from them, too. Point out that you have some new technical knowledge and skills that will make their jobs easier. Make it an offer, not an order. Don't push so hard."

Andrew looked down at his shoes. " 'Yellow sneaker syndrome,' huh?"

Paul nodded. "It happens to every new supervisor."

"Did it happen to you?"

"Sure. How do you think I found out about it?"

It's possible, even likely, you have some young people like Andrew in supervisory roles. Though smaller in numbers, the twentysomething crowd is better educated. Those members of this generation who are especially ambitious will find many opportunities to develop as managers.

What they bring in terms of higher education is often offset by a lack of real-world experience. Sometimes, maybe more frequently than we realize, they are placed in positions of authority for which they are woefully prepared. Not yet able to focus on the new challenges and responsibilities of managing people, the twentysomething supervisor may wind up, metaphorically of course, with "yellow sneaker syndrome."

The best and the brightest tend to stand out. Their technical skills may allow them to really shine in comparison with their less-gifted peers. Performing well makes twentysomething employees particularly visible. They may appear more skilled than they actually are. A manager casting about for someone to fill that vacant supervisory position may well reason, "Why not? She's young, but she knows her way around information systems. She can pick up management skills along the way. Besides, she's so good with people!"

In this chapter we help you prepare the young supervisor for that first managerial responsibility. As the more experienced leader, you have both the responsibility and the opportunity to help your fledgling supervisor get off on the right foot.

As a new supervisor, the twentysomething employee will face some unique challenges. Obviously, not everyone will be pleased with the idea that a younger worker has been promoted to management.

This chapter examines four key challenges facing the new supervisor: supervising friends, supervising employees who are older, handling employees who resent the new supervisor, and supervising employees who are younger than the twentysomething supervisor. We also cite common new-supervisor mistakes. We discuss the importance of becoming a mentor to your new young supervisor. We conclude the chapter by offering specific techniques and tools you can use to help ease the transition from worker to supervisor.

Change and Transition

When a worker of any age leaves the worker ranks and takes on the role of supervision, his work life is changed dramatically. The change from employee to manager is more than just a shift in title. The individual's personal as well as professional life is deeply affected.

Organizations, typically, don't understand the difference between change and transition. William Bridges, in his excellent book, *Surviving Corporate Transition,* argues that organizational change has a profound effect on the individual:

> "We do not foresee or know what to do with the psychological effects of change on people. We are unprepared when the changes we make disorient people and leave them demoralized, self-absorbed, and full of mistrust."[2]

In our experience, organizations take a straight-line approach to change. A date is set for the twentysomething worker to begin the new role as supervisor. The date arrives, and by some kind of magic the person is transformed. She left work on Friday a member of labor and she came back on Monday a member of management. Although the change has occurred, the transition is just beginning. Every new beginning starts with an ending. The individual will pass through seven phases in this transition time: denial, anger, bargaining, depression, acceptance, reconstruction, and congruence.[3]

Denial: "Hey, not me! I don't want to be anybody's boss!"

The new supervisor may actually deny that he is qualified to take on the mantle of leadership. "Who, me?" he may ask incredulously. Denial is a natural response to change, especially unexpected change.

Anger: "Oh, come on! I hate it when the company does something like this."

We discuss this in greater detail a bit further on. Let us just say now that this is a common response to change—even the good news of a promotion to supervisor. Anger may be expressed by those around the new supervisor or even by the supervisor herself.

Bargaining: "Is it okay if I keep my desk out here where I'm with the old gang?"

This phase occurs when the inevitable is realized: the change has actually occurred. The person in this phase will look for ways to keep things as they were. "Can I still be with my friends if I'm the supervisor?"

Depression: "This just isn't working out. I'll never be a good manager."

When transition occurs, there are many emotional ups and downs. One of the emotions experienced in the down cycle is depression. The new supervisor may wonder why in the world she ever agreed to the promotion. She begins to understand that leadership is difficult and that no matter what she does somebody isn't going to like it.

As the new supervisor begins to pass through the gray zone of transition, he begins to accept the new state of affairs. Here is an important point for you to understand: *acceptance does not equal commitment.* In this phase the twentysomething is in the first stages of moving toward a fully functioning state of handling the new role. He's not there yet.

Reconstruction: "Well, I'm still struggling, but I can see light at the end of the tunnel."
The twentysomething begins behaving differently. "I think I'm going to like this new role" would be a statement indicating movement through the reconstruction phase. At this point the individual is beginning to reconstruct her reality to match the new role she has assumed.

Congruence: "I know what I have to do and I'm ready to get on with it."
This is the final phase and it marks the point of buy-in. When the twentysomething reaches this phase, he has entered a state of commitment to the new role. But don't assume that means there will be no problems or mistakes. Much learning will still need to be done. However, the person in this phase has brought into congruence his previous role as employee and the new role of supervisor.

The wise leader will recognize these phases as normal and natural to the change and transition process. Organizations cause problems for their employees when they insist change be accomplished in the straight-line method and do not recognize the very critical psychological need for people to pass through the transition phases.

A very common phenomenon that occurs during times of personal or organizational transition is that people invent all kinds of ways to maintain the status quo—even when it doesn't work very well. Some people, it seems, prefer certain misery to uncertain change. Nature offers an interesting fact: when clams are removed from the ocean and flown across the country to a restaurant they continue to open and close on their old tidal schedules right up to the minute they get into hot water. When it comes to making changes, some people are like clams.

Four Key Challenges

New supervisors face many challenges. They may have to supervise former peers and friends. There may be older and more experienced employees who believe they should have gotten the supervisor's job. Other twentysomething workers will look at the new young supervisor as a peer rather than manager. There will be those who openly resist the leadership efforts of the new supervisor. You can help your twentysomething supervisors by understanding the following four key challenges and by helping them to successfully meet each of them.

Challenge One: Supervising Friends
One of the first challenges your twentysomething supervisor will face is the very real possibility of supervising friends. One day they were peers, buddies, and coworkers, and the next day, one of them is in management. The peer pressure felt by the young supervisor can be immense. Her friends may exhibit one or more of the following emotional responses: mad, sad, glad, or scared.

The Mad Response.
Some of the new supervisor's friends will direct anger toward their peer. This is often one of the first reactions to organizational change. Their anger may stem from the fact that they themselves were not chosen. It may also occur as they realize that the friend will now have more privileges and, usually, more money. They may experience anger as they become aware that their former peer will now have something to say about performance appraisals and compensation decisions. You will recognize this as one of the seven phases in the transition cycle we discussed above.

What peers might say: "Oh, great! Now that you're a supervisor I suppose you'll get a big head and start bossing us around. I guess the only way to get ahead around here is to kiss up to management. This really ticks me off."

What the new supervisor should say: "I understand you're angry. Maybe I would be too, in your position. Your anger is natural and normal and I accept it. The fact is, I'm the supervisor now and we have to continue working together."

The Sad Response.
For some employees, a sense of sadness may prevail for a time. A feeling of loss and abandonment may occur as they watch their friend pack up and prepare to move into a larger, perhaps nicer, work space. Change in one person's life—in this case the new supervisor's--often creates feelings of loss. Many people view change as having something taken away rather than something added. The sadness on the part of the supervisor and his peers may come from a perceived loss of camaraderie with the newly promoted friend. They see their friend moving on while they stay in place. The new supervisor is drawn back to the past while simultaneously feeling pushed into the future.

What peers might say: "How will we ever be able to go on without you? Can't you still stay with us? Do you have to move into that office? I'll miss you!"

What the new supervisor should say: "It's not like I won't be around you. We can still go for coffee and lunch. It's important that I have a private space now because as a supervisor I'll sometimes have to discuss confidential matters. Let's go have coffee and discuss this some more."

The Glad Response.
Just as some of the twentysomething supervisor's friends will be mad or sad, some will be glad. Some will cheer on the good fortune of their colleague while realizing that a new relationship is being defined. There is excitement and anticipation associated with the new promotion. This is a positive and supportive response.

But another kind of "glad response" can cause problems. In this scenario, the coworker is glad for her friend's promotion to management for a different, ulterior reason. The friend's expectation is that the buddy relationship can go on, undisturbed. The twentysomething supervisor must clarify the relationship immediately.

What peers might say: "Gee, Carlos, it's great you've been made a supervisor. Together we can really have the inside track on things around here. You'll get all the inside scoop from management and I'll keep tabs on what's going on with the other employees, so we should have it made!"

What the new supervisor should say: "Our relationship has to be different now. We should preserve our friendship. But we now have to separate business from social life. I'll need your help. Let's agree that during business hours we're professional colleagues and that we won't discuss confidential matters during our social time together."

The Scared Response.
Friends and coworkers of the new twentysomething supervisor may have other fears. Their fears may be based on a belief that this friend will somehow take advantage of past shared confidences. Those who are not friends of the new supervisor may fear that former friends will receive favored treatment. Friends may fear that their new supervisor will go out of her way to avoid favoritism and will stick them with an undeserved amount of dirty work in order to demonstrate objectivity. When employees feel vulnerable, they are likely to experience the emotion of fear.

What peers might say: "I'm really scared now that you're going to be my supervisor. We had all those heart-to-heart talks. You know a lot about me that others don't. You know my strengths and my weaknesses. I hope I'll be okay."

What the new supervisor should say: "You're going to be okay. It's natural to feel some fear. I know I would if the situation were reversed. We've had a lot of trust in the past and that's our strength. What you've said to me in confidence in the past will be kept confidential. I'll treat you like I treat others. If I don't, let me know."

HOW YOU, THE LEADER, CAN HELP

You can help your young supervisor to prepare for the mad, sad, glad, and scared responses. Take time to counsel the twentysome-thing supervisor before the promotion is announced. Help her think through and identify all the possible reactions friends may have. Here are some statements and questions to help guide you in this counseling.

Ask your new supervisor:

1. How are you feeling about the idea of being a supervisor?
2. What concerns or fears do you have about supervising other people?
3. Have you thought about what it will be like to supervise your friends?
4. Let's list some of the possible reactions they might have.
5. What do you plan to say when they state their reactions?
6. How can I, as your manager, help you get ready to supervise your friends?

The twentysomething supervisor will probably experience a certain amount of fear and ambiguity. Help him talk through concerns with you. Encourage him to sit down with friends and to make agreements about this new relationship. Managing these expectations from the outset will help the new supervisor learn to lead friends with a minimum of problems.

Challenge Two: Supervising Older or More Experienced Employees
This can be a touchy one. When a young person is placed in a leadership role over older and/or more experienced employees,

fireworks can start. The young supervisor may be treated as a son or daughter by the older employee. Sometimes her skills are discredited by employees with more experience.

If you know your young supervisor is going to be thrust into any of these situations, it is imperative you prepare her adequately.

Scenario: The older employees don't take the young supervisor seriously. One of our management seminar participants was a very bright twenty-four-year-old computer technician. She completed her college degree in night school while working full time for her company. She didn't anticipate that her career would take a turn toward management. When the supervisor quit, she was promoted to fill the vacancy. Here's how she expressed her frustration:

> I was made a supervisor because I'm the only one who knows how our new computer system works. I have to direct four men—all of them old enough to be my father. They're very nice to me and that's the problem. They won't take me seriously! When I try to get them to do something or try something new, they smile, or wink at me, call me "honey," and then they do whatever they want to do instead.

Here's what we suggested:

1. Meet with each of the four men privately. Acknowledge your relative youth for the position you hold.
2. Verbally acknowledge their loyalty, longevity, and experience.
3. Describe, as objectively as possible, the behaviors that cause problems.
4. Explain how those behaviors affect productivity.
5. Ask for a specific change in behavior.
6. State the positive consequences if they change this behavior ("We'll all be able to get our work done more efficiently and productively").

Older and/or more experienced workers sometimes have a tendency to adopt younger workers and supervisors and to act in a parental role—sometimes nurturing, sometimes criticizing. The new supervisor must not allow herself to be cast into the role of adoptable child.

HOW YOU, THE LEADER, CAN HELP

It's likely you can speak from the perspective of the older or more experienced employee. You've been there. Consider the six steps we offered above as a way of coaching the new supervisor. You might help by letting him rehearse or play roles with you to practice what he will need to say to the older employees.

Challenge Three: Supervising Resistant Employees

As we noted earlier, a certain amount of denial and anger are common when organizations are thrust into the milieu of change and transition. This challenge is especially troublesome for the new young supervisor because it involves conflict—something most of us try to avoid. Problems may occur when others are passed by for promotion, especially if they were actual candidates under consideration. Sometimes the resistance is born of jealousy.

Employees may express their resentment with such behaviors as:

- slowing down work.
- making "mistakes."
- giving negative verbal messages and nonverbal signals.
- "forgetting" how to do things they knew how to do before.
- showing open hostility toward the new supervisor.
- being insubordinate.
- spreading rumors.
- complaining to higher-ranking managers.

Jerry, a twentysomething supervisor for one of our clients, nervously faced his team of workers. Six weeks earlier they had been shifted from another department and put under Jerry's supervision. With the exception of one or two individuals, they had formed a tight clique and had banded together to resist the new supervisor. After conferring with Tom, his boss, Jerry called a special meeting. As consultants to the organization, we were present. His message to the group went something like this:

> I know some of you are unhappy that I was chosen to be a supervisor. I'm twenty-five and I look like I'm about eighteen. It's a constant problem for me. I'm also aware that you didn't want to be transferred to my unit. If I were you, I'd probably feel the same way. Anyway, I've observed that some of the work is not getting done as efficiently and effectively as it should be. Specifically (here he cited several well-documented examples).
>
> You know, we all have to work together. It's not necessary that we like one another. But let me be perfectly clear. I will neither tolerate nor allow any deviation from previous performance levels. Each of you is a capable, responsible human being. I trust you to do the best work you know how to do. To do less would be to dishonor yourselves, not me.
>
> Please join me in a cooperative effort to make our unit the pride of the company. I promise I will be fair and give an open ear to all points of view. By working together, all our jobs will be easier. Thank you. The meeting is adjourned.

We were struck by the eloquence of the young man's statement. We've not done it justice here, but we hope you get the point. Sometimes the best approach to conflict is to confront the source head-on, as Jerry did. In case you're wondering, his group began to work as a team.

HOW YOU, THE LEADER, CAN HELP
One of the most important actions you can take is to model appropriate conflict management behaviors with your twentysomething

supervisors and employees. They observe you constantly and take their cues from you. Manage your own conflicts productively. Let your subordinates know that conflict is normal and natural, and that it is absolutely necessary for creativity to flourish. But also impress upon them the fact that unmanaged or destructive conflict can be a detriment to the group and its productivity.

Help the young supervisor polish her conflict confrontation skills. There are many good workshops and seminars on this subject. For a nominal amount of money you will equip your twentysomething with both leadership and management skills with high payoffs.

Finally, let your young supervisor know that sometimes the best way to deal with resistant employees is to confront them with their behaviors. *The key is to focus on observable behaviors, not "attitudes."* Attitudes cannot be seen. They are internal. All that can be observed are behaviors. Keep confrontation constructive by focusing on behaviors and using a "let's solve the problem together" approach.

Challenge Four: Supervising Younger Employees
This challenge, among the four we've discussed, is unique. The young supervisor may be leading employees who are even younger than himself. There are positive aspects to this challenge. One of the more obvious is the closeness in age between supervisor and subordinate. Another advantage the twentysomething supervisor has is that he probably shares key value systems with the younger employees.

Here are some important "do's" and "don'ts." Pass these on to your twentysomething supervisor:

Do:

- Have faith that your younger employees can do a good job.
- Give them projects for which they can take ownership.
- Give younger employees close supervision until they are "with the program."

157

- Provide as much freedom and autonomy as you can.
- Check regularly on their progress.
- Be certain they understand directions or instructions.
- Praise them frequently when they take steps in the right direction.
- Be visible and available to them when they need your help.

Don't:

- Think that just because they're young you can't give them responsibility.
- Try to do everything yourself.
- Tell them how to do everything.
- Put so many controls on them they can't exercise initiative.
- Constantly check on them.
- Assume they understand your directions or instructions.
- Correct their errors or mistakes in front of their peers.
- Expect them to be fully independent of supervision.

HOW YOU, THE LEADER, CAN HELP

Modeling appropriate leadership behavior is probably the most important example you can set for your subordinates. Be ready to give them some tips like those listed above. Let them know they aren't expected to know everything and that it is okay to say "I don't know" without losing credibility.

These four challenges facing the twentysomething supervisor appear common in many organizations, judging by our conversations with hundreds of managers throughout the country. We hear them mentioned frequently in our workshops and seminars.

Mistake Management

People will make mistakes and the young supervisor is no exception. We thought you'd be interested in some of the statements we've heard from managers in our national workshops:

Common Mistakes New Young Supervisors Make

1. They try to make too many changes too fast.
2. They have unrealistic expectations about their ability to manage.
3. They self-destruct by worrying too much about being liked.
4. They let older workers intimidate them.
5. They run to the boss for advice instead of making decisions and taking the consequences.
6. They get on a power or ego trip and wind up making the people around them angry or disgusted.
7. They worry too much about their age and forget about their incredible talent.
8. They try to be buddies with their employees.
9. They don't nip discipline problems in the bud.
10. They get hung up on rules and procedures—they're inflexible.

HOW YOU, THE LEADER, CAN HELP

Let your young supervisors know that mistakes are inevitable. Mistakes need to be seen as learning experiences. *Forbes* reprinted excerpts from a speech by British comedian and film star John Cleese titled, "The Importance of Mistakes." Cleese, whose company produces management training videos, spoke on the need to allow for mistakes:

> In an organization where mistakes are not allowed, you get two types of counterproductive behavior. First, since mistakes are "bad" if they're committed by people at the top, the feedback arising from those mistakes has to be ignored in order that those top people can pretend that no mistake has been made. So it doesn't get fixed. Second, if they're committed by people lower down in the organization, mistakes get concealed.[4]

As a leader, give your twentysomethings the freedom and dignity to practice getting better. That's what mistake management is all about. Of course, mistakes cannot be allowed to occur indefinitely. Each mistake by the young supervisor should serve as a step to better and more effective leadership. Careful coaching and counseling by you will begin to lay the groundwork for improvement.

Become a Mentor

The new young supervisor will benefit greatly from being mentored. What is a mentor and how do you become one? A mentor is someone who becomes an adviser, coach, and confidant to a subordinate. By its nature, mentorship is synonymous with sponsorship.

The mentor "sponsors" the person being mentored. She keeps a watchful eye out for the "mentee"—the one being mentored. The mentee develops a strong bond of trust with the mentor. Advice is freely given when requested. Knowledge is shared. Successes by the mentee are mutually celebrated. Problems are discussed and means of solving them are considered together.

The mentor opens doors in the organization for the one being mentored. Helping him get involved in projects with high visibility would be an example of mentor sponsorship. The mentor has the best welfare of the mentee in mind at all times. This is not favoritism. This is part of the necessary learning on the job that new supervisors must have to be successful. They need another authority figure to emulate.

Being a mentor can be time consuming. The day will come when you no longer need or want to mentor the person. This is a healthy moment in the relationship because it indicates the mentee's growing confidence and ability to manage herself. Some experts in mentor relationships say that the partnership should be ended at the first sign that the mentee can fly on her own. To go beyond that point, they argue, is to create a dysfunctional codependency between the two.

How do you become a mentor? Well, you probably don't have to take any specific action. You don't need to send out notices proclaiming "mentor available." The way it usually happens is that some young supervisor will find himself coming to you frequently for advice and discussion. That might be how the relationship begins. Being a mentor can be immensely rewarding, both to the mentor and to the mentored one. Passing on one's skills and knowledge to help another grow professionally and personally is a particularly fine gift from a leader.

TAKING ACTION

A positive self-image is essential to a successful leader. New supervisors often operate from a self-esteem deficit. It's as if they've "maxed out" on their self-worth credit limit. While it's true that self-esteem, by definition, must come from within the individual, here are twenty actions you can take that will contribute powerfully to your young supervisor's sense of self-worth.

1. Make sure you say, "Good morning. How are you?" or an appropriate greeting every day. Don't forget to wait for an answer.
2. Tell them immediately when they've done a good job. Point out what they did, specifically, that you appreciate.
3. Acknowledge and encourage them in their outside interests.
4. Share an example of a mistake you once made and how you learned from it.
5. Listen. Put down your pen. Turn toward him or her. Get fully engaged in the act of listening.
6. Share information whenever you can.
7. Take them out for coffee or lunch once in a while. Let them take their turn buying.
8. Acknowledge their ideas in front of others.
9. Send them copies of articles, cartoons, or book reviews that might interest them.
10. Repeat compliments you've heard about them.
11. Ask them to make a short presentation or to plan a meeting. Let them attend with you and introduce them to others.
12. When you need to offer criticism, tell them how they can do better next time. Help them use their mistakes as opportunities for insight and growth.
13. Take their ideas seriously.
14. Send them birthday and special occasion cards. Surprise them once in a while with an unexpected card or silly gift.

15. Attach a Post-it note to their paycheck with a "Thank You" message.
16. Ask for their help.
17. Treat them with dignity and respect.
18. Be visible and available.
19. Be a mentor.
20. Treat them as human beings and individuals of worth.

Notes

1. Gene Perret, *Funny Business,* Prentice Hall, Englewood Cliffs, N.J., 1990, p. 22.
2. William Bridges, *Surviving Corporate Transition,* Doubleday, New York, 1988, p. 7.
3. Elisabeth Kübler-Ross, in *On Death and Dying* was the first to label the phases of denial, anger, bargaining, depression and acceptance. Kübler-Ross argues that terminally-ill patients experience these emotional phases as they approach death. We have modified Kübler-Ross's phases and added "reconstruction" and "congruence." We certainly don't equate supervising people with terminal illness. However, the phases provide a useful way at looking at the grieving process people must be allowed to experience when organizations thrust them into change and transition.
4. Quoted in *Video Arts In the Press,* a publication of Video Arts Inc., Northbrook, Illinois. The *Forbes* article appeared in the May 16, 1988, issue.

CHAPTER-AT-A-GLANCE

• Organizations and their managers typically don't understand the difference between change and transition. They impose changes unilaterally, while those most affected by the changes must work their way through a process of transition.

• When individuals are thrust into transition they pass through seven phases: denial, anger, bargaining, depression, acceptance, reconstruction and congruence.

• The twentysomething supervisor faces four unique challenges: supervising peers and friends, older or more experienced employees, resistant employees, and younger employees.

• Young supervisors, like everyone, make mistakes. Give the twentysomething supervisor freedom to make mistakes and guidance to learn from them.

• Leaders can provide powerful modeling examples by mentoring young supervisors.

The quality and the motivating issues are the two Achilles' heels of temporary help.
—Richard Belous, Labor Economist

10

Here Today, Gone Tomorrow: Temporary and Seasonal Workers

Here's a horror story for you. Corroon and Black Corporation recently hired a temporary worker to fold 80,000 insurance certificates and stuff them into envelopes. Within a few days, someone found thousands of the certificates and envelopes in a freight elevator. Tired and bored with the project, the temporary had found a creative solution to cut her workload.[1]

For many industries, it is a necessity to hire temporary and seasonal workers: L. L. Bean hires employees to work a few months at Christmas time; Keck, Mahin & Cate, a Chicago law firm, hires temporary clerical workers for particularly time-consuming cases, some of which last for as long as a year; Johnson & Johnson hires contractors to analyze its subsidiaries. Resorts, restaurants, and retailers of all description have come to depend more and more on temporaries.

As companies get rid of layers of management and become leaner, it makes more sense to turn to temporary employees when the work stacks up. In fact, part-time, contract, and temporary workers now constitute nearly one-third of the U.S. workforce.[2] The workers tend to range in age from eighteen to twenty-four; the average age is twenty-two. They perform a wide range of jobs, depending on age and experience, and offer unique challenges to the supervisor in charge.

WHY COMPANIES ARE TURNING TO TEMPORARY WORKERS

To alleviate an overload of work	70%
For special projects	61
To cover for workers on leave	52
To cover for vacationing workers	51
To fill in for departing workers	44
To fill in for sick employees	37
To perform duties where permanent jobs aren't financially justified	36

Source: *The Wall Street Journal*, July 16, 1990. Reprinted by permission of *The Wall Street Journal*, © 1990, Dow Jones and Co., Inc. All rights reserved worldwide.

TEMPORARY, PART-TIME AND SEASONAL WORKERS IN THE U.S.

	1980	1986	
	(in millions)		*Increase*
Part-timers	16.3	19.5	20%
Self-employed	8.5	9.2	9
Temporaries	.4	.7	75
Other	3.3	4.8	45

Source: *The Wall Street Journal*, July 16, 1990. Reprinted by permission of *The Wall Street Journal*, © 1990, Dow Jones and Co., Inc. All rights reserved worldwide.

If you supervise temporaries, you'll find lots of helpful information in this chapter. We'll start by zeroing in on the inherent challenges of working with nonpermanent employees. Then we'll share some fascinating information about what motivates them. You'll get acquainted with the "theory of expectancy," which may change the way you set standards. Finally, we'll offer you nine solutions that are uniquely applicable to this special segment of our workforce.

The Problems

According to the managers we've talked with, here are the key issues involved in working with temporary, seasonal, and contract employees:

- Their managers tend to have low expectations of them.
- Quality—you simply don't know if you can count on them the way you count on your full-time employees.
- Their work ethic is different—even from the typical twentysomething worker's.
- Managers expect much less loyalty from temporaries.
- Hiring, training, and orienting temporaries is expensive.
- What motivates the full-time employee—promotions and raises—often fails to motivate the temporary worker.

What *Does* Motivate Them

Bill Hill, management professor for Colorado Mountain College in Steamboat Springs, Colorado, became interested in seasonal workers in the 1980s. He has traveled internationally, working with corporations which hire predominantly, and sometimes exclusively, seasonal workers. Hill cites two case studies based on actual situations his clients have encountered with seasonal workers:

Case Study 1*
Susan Jones, age twenty-two, from Des Moines, is a seasonal sales representative in a Steamboat Springs, Colorado, ski shop. She graduated from Iowa State University last spring, with a degree in English literature. She is an avid skier and backpacker and would like to reside permanently in Colorado.

Susan came to Steamboat in November and accepted a seasonal job in hopes of finding a more permanent job in the resort community. The ski season and her job will end in about four weeks. So far, she has been unable to find a summer job. If she isn't successful in finding a job, she will probably return to Des Moines and try again next fall.

Like a lot of her ski buddies, Susan is very bright, athletic, and

*Reprinted with permission. © Bill Hill.

personable. She's definitely a people person, but she dislikes authority and sometimes lacks self-motivation. Her work habits might be described as flexible, especially on powder ski days.

Susan has been a good worker, most of the time. But now that ski season is coming to an end, she's starting to slack off and has called in sick three of the last seven work days. Some of her coworkers are doing the same. You suspect it could be spring (skiing) fever.

As her supervisor, what would you do, especially considering the fact there are few replacements available in the season? Business is busy.

*Case Study 2**
Sam Smith, from Kansas, came to work for you in November. As soon as ski season ends, he plans to go to Arizona for two weeks, then back home to Kansas to work on his father's farm. He's twenty years old, and this is his first job away from home. He came to Vail with three friends, two of whom have already quit and returned home.

Sam has been a good worker, except for a bit of burnout in mid-January. Growing up on a farm, he knows how to work and is determined to complete the season.

Nevertheless, with three weeks to go in the season, Sam is starting to slow down and is acting a little cynical about the job. He also isn't being a good team worker and has been complaining a lot about housing conditions. Some of the other employees are complaining about his attitude.

What would you do?

Hill's research shows that temporary and seasonal workers are not motivated by the same factors as traditional, year-round employees. For five years, he has conducted a yearly twenty-question survey of

*Reprinted with permission. ©Bill Hill.

seasonal and permanent workers. Here are the results of his 1990 survey:

MOTIVATING FACTORS FOR SEASONAL WORKERS

What is most important in a job?

1. Pay and fringe benefits.
2. Recognition for good work.
3. People I work with.
4. Learning new skills.
5. Job security.

Last year's survey was the first in which money appeared in the number one slot. In all previous years, "recognition for good work" and "learning new skills" ranked first and second. "Pay and fringe benefits," in each of the four preceding years, ranked dead last. This seems to suggest that seasonal workers in the nineties are primarily concerned with survival. Hill's advice to managers and supervisors is to take a good look at pay scales and cost of living, making certain you are paying your temporaries enough to live on, given the current cost of living.

Disneyland

If you're a manager working with seasonal employees in the service industry, you'll want to examine the Disney model. The bulk of its employees are hourly high school and college students. "Human resources personnel deal with hourly employees who have varying degrees of expertise" along with "salaried professionals who are responsible for jobs ranging from creative design of the theme parks to financial wizards who dream up new projects."[3] Disney has a unique style of hiring, training, and motivating hourly employees to do routine chores. Their style is not for everyone—some twentysomethings will find it too rigid—but it has earned Disney the reputation as a leader in the service industry.

Here's what they do at Disney to manage and motivate workers:

1. Every worker knows the company's mission.
Disney's mission is to make their Guests (always with a capital *G*) happy. It's just that simple. All those who work for Disney, from management to the people who sweep the streets, understand that mission.

2. Every worker sees his or her role in the company's mission.
Disney was founded on the principle that you can't make other people happy if you aren't *acting* happy. Therefore, Disney is not a business; it's a performance. Employees are called cast members and are hired by Central Casting. They are coached extensively on how to perform their roles by trainers and mentors following a director/actor model.

Everyone at Disney knows his or her performance affects the company's mission. Red Pope, "a long-time Disney observer," asked his own teenagers, working in Orlando, why they were going through so much training to be ticket-takers. His teens replied, "What happens if someone wants to know where the restrooms are? . . . We need to know the answers. . . . Our job every minute is to help Guests enjoy the party."[4]

3. Training and development are essential.
Disney's hiring, orientation, and training programs are the most extensive of any company we know. Potential employees tend to self-screen because of Disney's well-known reputation for conservatism. During the application procedure, prospective employees view a movie that acquaints them with the company culture—dress code, rules, and policies. An interviewer meets with a group of three potential employees to evaluate their human relations and communications skills. The way a candidate treats other candidates probably reflects the way he or she will treat Guests and coworkers.

During an eight-hour orientation, new hires learn about the Disney culture, its history, and philosophy. The orientation and training program is constantly revamped; each year, it is modified based on feedback from supervisors and employees. "Cast members" receive between eight and forty-eight hours of training after orientation and before they go to work. Then there are all sorts of learning opportunities available—from career counseling to classes in interviewing and goal-setting.[5]

4. There is an informality about authority.
All managers spend several days each year away from their offices, dressed in costume, serving hamburgers, taking tickets, loading people onto rides, and performing other roles their workers perform.[6] Everyone, including the president, wears a name tag with his first name only.[7]

5. Information is at each worker's fingertips.
At Disneyland and Disney World, hundreds of phones are located throughout the park near work stations. The phones are direct hotlines to a Question-and-Answer service that provides employees with information they need to offer truly exceptional service.[8]

The Theory of Expectancy

Perhaps the biggest problem in managing young seasonal workers has to do with setting expectations for them. The theory of expectancy says people live up to what we expect from them. Bill Hill likes to use seasonal workers at ski resorts to demonstrate this theory. Traditionally, they've been referred to as "ski bums." Hill believes such a name sets clear expectations, and not positive ones. "If we call them ski bums," he says, "we are sending a clear message that we expect them to behave like bums." On the contrary, if we want them to behave like professionals, we need to refer to them as professionals, treat them as professionals, and give them professional challenges and training. "We need to professionalize their jobs and set high expectations. As soon as we professionalize our attitudes toward them and the jobs they perform, we will have professional seasonal workers."

Hill offers an example of how careful examination and the restructuring of expectations can affect recruitment: Two directly competing businesses in the resort town of Steamboat Springs, Colorado, were recruiting workers for the busy Christmas season. One company could not find anyone to hire, while the other had eager prospective workers constantly at its door. Hill's backyard research revealed that the company with the eager recruits treated people as professionals, not as ski bums. "They had a philosophy of treating their workers as people, and offered them skills and training they could use the rest of their lives."

After some negative experiences with contract workers, John Younker, vice president of the American Productivity Center in Houston, decided to invest time with his temporary employees, spelling out expectations, developing task lists, discussing work preferences, outlining the project, and teaching evaluation standards. In short, Younker spends time setting clear expectations and making his contract workers feel a sense of ownership in their projects.[9]

The theory of expectancy is critical when leading temporary and seasonal workers. As you'll see in chapter eleven, it makes a difference to all twentysomethings. Our next chapter, "Letter to a Manager," was written by Jo Leda Martin, a twenty-five-year-old worker. She shares her thoughts on growing up in the seventies, her first working years, and the type of leadership she prefers.

TAKING ACTION

When we discuss temporary and seasonal workers with managers in our seminars, we find their biggest concern is: how can we keep them coming back year after year? Here's what we've found to be effective:

1. *Capitalize on peer pressure and teamwork, especially with seasonal workers.*

   When members of the team do something wrong, they let the team down. Then the team—not the boss—deals with the problem. The boss's role is to set expectations and then to let the team go out and have a good time getting the job done.

   After the freight elevator incident at Corroon and Black, managers decided to hire more than one temp so they could keep one another company. Consequently, all the materials were mailed on time.[10]

2. *Don't take the "work ethic" for granted.*

   Some temporary workers simply don't understand the importance of being on time—and other principles we take for granted. Your young temporaries may not be well grounded in basic work standards. Take time in the beginning to discuss your norms: schedule, attitude, appearance.

3. *Review your pay scale.*

   Are you paying enough to keep up with the cost of living and support a decent quality of life?

4. *Use praise freely.*

   Be tough on standards and expectations, but let your temporaries know you care about them.

5. *Set high standards.*

   Many managers feel they have to lower standards for non-permanent workers. Bill Hill disagrees. "Don't lower your standards. If anything, make them higher and tougher.

When you expect professionalism, employees tend to live up to that expectation."

6. *Provide training and career counseling.*

Look at seasonal employees as people who want career advancement. Let them know how the skills they learn will help them in their future. At Johnson and Johnson, contract workers are introduced to executives they can turn to for references when they've performed well.[11]

7. *Treat them like full-time employees.*

At Corroon and Black, managers see to it that temporaries receive memos that relate to their work. They get nameplates and have their own restroom keys. Temporaries even participate on the in-house volleyball team.[12]

8. *Think "kaizen."*

This Japanese management theory means "the spirit of continuous improvement." One of the secrets of Japanese business, kaizen translates into daily growth for each worker. Nearly all young employees, especially temporaries, want to improve. As a leader, start your day asking yourself, "How can I make today a growth opportunity for my people? How can I excite and challenge them?"

Notes

1. Michael J. McCarthy, "Managers Face Dilemma with 'Temps,' " *Wall Street Journal,* July 16, 1990.
2. Ibid.
3. Charlene Marmer Solomon, "How Does Disney Do It?," *Personnel Journal,* December 1989, p. 53.
4. Thomas J. Peters and Robert H. Waterman, Jr., *In Search of Excellence,* Warner Books, 1982, pp. 167 and 168.
5. Solomon, p. 55.
6. Ibid., pp. 54 and 55.
7. Peters and Waterman, p. 167.

CHAPTER-AT-A-GLANCE

- As companies grow leaner, it makes sense to turn to temporary employees when the work stacks up.

- Temporary workers make up nearly one-third of the American workforce.

- Managers have low expectations of temps and seasonals.

- Temporary and seasonal workers have a different work ethic and are motivated differently than regular employees.

- Hiring, training, and orienting them is expensive.

- Seasonal workers in a 1990 survey ranked the top factors that motivate them: pay and fringe benefits, recognition, and relationships with coworkers.

- The Disney model operates like this:
  Every worker knows the company's mission.
  Every worker sees his or her role.
  Training and development are essential.
  There is an informality about authority.
  Information is at each worker's fingertips.

- Practice the theory of expectancy with temporary and seasonal workers.

- To keep them coming back year after year:
  Use praise freely.
  Set high standards.
  Provide training and career counseling.
  Treat them like full-time employees.
  Think "kaizen."

8. Ibid., p. 122.
9. Ibid., p. 168.
10. McCarthy.
11. Ibid.
12. Ibid.

11

Letter to a Manager

By Jo Leda Martin

Dear Manager:

I want to begin this chapter by telling you what it is not. This chapter is not the voice of all young workers. The information here is not the accumulation of statistical data from surveys of thousands of young workers. It is not a representative sampling of how *all* young workers feel about work, managers, and motivation. It should not be interpreted as a broad generalization of what all young workers believe and value. This chapter is the voice of one young worker only.

The purpose of this chapter is to make a request of you and all managers: get to know us, the young workers, each for who we are. We are not all alike. You can manage us more effectively when you know us. Take the time to learn what our differences are and then put your knowledge about each of us to work for you.

So, let me tell you about one young worker. About who I am and my background. Because I believe that who young workers are as individuals, not as a population, affects what types of jobs we want, what types of managers we enjoy working for, what motivates us, and what we value. Ultimately for you, my manager, this knowledge

This entire chapter was written by Jo Leda Martin, a well-spoken representative of the twentysomething generation.

177

about me will improve your ability to manage me effectively.

Douglas Stewart, author of *The Power of People Skills,* contends that "the greatest consistent source of power over the ages has been knowledge. Even if large armies could temporarily hold power, smart armies with more recent technology and information soon prevailed."[1] Knowledge is power. Get to know us. It *will* make a difference.

Who I Am

I would like to create a mental picture for you of the young worker who is writing. I am female, twenty-five years old, and I have been out of college for almost three years. I have had three positions since graduation: I began in fund-raising; I then acted as training manager for a corporate travel agency; now I hold my current position. Three positions in three years may cause you to wonder. I moved out from each of these positions to take on new responsibilities. Each offered me more opportunity for growth and advancement, and was more in line with my career goals. Currently, I am a training coordinator for a management training and consulting firm.

How I Grew Up

I believe that people parent the way they were parented, and that they manage the way they were parented. Many people in my generation were parented differently from the generations of several of our managers and supervisors. If this belief is true, it is important for a manager to know how his or her young worker grew up. Perhaps your style of managing and parenting is not the style the young worker is accustomed to. Perhaps, worst of all, that particular style will only fail to motivate your young employee and succeed at creating a great deal of frustration for you.

I, like many of my peers, was a latchkey kid. I came home to an empty house, had to put myself to bed, and get myself ready for school, often alone. I learned good common sense at an early age because I had to. I'm glad of that. I knew the difference between recognizing that a burner was hot and laying my hand on top of it. Seldom did my friends and I engage in destructive behavior. I had the responsibility to feed the cat, not set him on fire. Most of us latchkey kids were not raised in a "hand-holding" environment. We were raised, for the most part, with firm lessons between right and wrong, faith in our ability to do the right thing, and a great, great deal of trust. There were not always warm baked cookies when we got home from school, but, often, warm notes:

> I hope you had a good day at school. Call me when you get home. Your dinner is ready in the refrigerator. It just needs a little warming. Do your homework and I'll be home around 8:30 P.M. I love you. Call me if you need anything, and please feed the cat.
>
> Mom

Being alone in an empty house is a big responsibility for a child. I was given a great deal of trust, autonomy, and independence. Someone was not always there to make sure I got my homework done. For the most part, I had to make sure I got it done myself. And I learned at a very young age the consequences for my actions and inactions. I did my homework not because my mom told me to, but because I knew what it felt like to be embarrassed by not having it done for class the next day. I took responsibility for my actions at a young age and for the consequences. My parents set high expectations for me, and gave me what I needed to live up to those expectations. Not out of fear, but out of choice. Not because they coddled me, but because they gave me the necessary information I needed to make good choices, and the freedom to make those choices. This is how I was parented, and how many of my peers from my generation were parented.

So how did this parenting style affect me as a young worker in the business world? Because of these experiences, I am independent and autonomous. I take responsibility for making sure that what I do, I do well. I take 100 percent of the responsibility when I fail, and 100 percent of the glory when I succeed. I know how to use good judgment, to take responsibility for my actions, behaviors, and choices, and to be held accountable for them.

My environment needs to begin as one of trust and empowerment, guidance and parameters, then autonomy and independence to carry through with my responsibilities and make decisions. By surrounding me and holding my hand, I feel that you don't trust that I can succeed. I begin to doubt myself, and make decisions not out of confidence in my ability, but out of fear. Then I do fail.

This is not a negative, but a benefit, to any manager who understands this about me, and about latchkey kids. Care, don't coddle; trust, don't suffocate. Don't fear that I'll do the wrong thing if you're not there, but have faith in my ability to make good, intelligent choices. Chances are with the latchkey kids, if you give us the ball and let us run with it down the court, we'll score. If you circle us, guard us, protect us, we may never get to the hoop and we'll probably give up trying.

Welcome to the Real World

Out of college, I felt like the rest of my peers—degree in hand, ready to conquer the business world. After being a finalist in several interviews with a variety of consumer products companies, as a sales representative, I was not hired. My hopes of taking the world by storm were quickly humbled. "I have a four-year degree, a 4.0 in my major, a 3.8 grade point average overall, was president of a national honor society, a nationally ranked speaker on one of the top ten speech teams in the country, and recipient of many scholarships and department awards in my major. Why won't they hire me?" I was deflated and frustrated.

Now, as I look back, not being hired for several months was, perhaps, a good thing. I learned a lot during those unemployed, out-of-college months. During that time I realized what it really meant to be young. In college, age didn't matter a whole lot, just integrity, capability, and willingness to learn. Not so in the real world of business. "A four-year degree does not an automatic job make."

I think that to businesses, a four-year degree just says that you can jump through hoops. Anyway, it is more of a prerequisite than a characteristic that causes you to stand apart from others.

I learned that right out of college, you *are* unskilled, young, just starting out. It is analogous to graduating from the sixth grade and having to start all over again in junior high. This was a never-ending cycle in school: starting over at the bottom again and having to slowly work your way up. Sound a lot like the real world of business? It never occurred to me that after college this cycle would continue.

As a senior in college, I was on top of the world, graduating with honors and accolades, and, all of a sudden, I felt like I was starting over again—the way I felt when I started junior high. I swallowed my pride, stuffed the accolades and honors deep down in my pocket, and pounded the pavement for a job. I did pull those accolades out often, though. I would read them to myself after receiving one of those rejection form letters:

> Dear Jiletta: [my name was never spelled right]
> Thank you for your application, but we do not have any positions available. We promise to keep your résumé in case, by some small miracle, we might want to hire you without any skills or prior work experience.

During that time, I also read a lot about the way managers perceive young workers. One perception is that our generation has had everything handed to us. We never had to work hard for anything. We don't appreciate an honest day's work. As I read this literature, I thought to myself, "They can't be talking about *me*, about *all* of us. Don't they realize how hard some of us are trying? How badly some of us want to work for them, to succeed as employees for them?" I worked hard to put myself through school, with dedication and commitment. I will give that same kind of hard work and dedication to any job I have. Out of school, I wanted a real job more than anything. I worked day and night searching and applying.

Now that I have been working for a few years, I know what it means to have a great person/job fit and the importance of finding not just a job, but a niche and a passion. I can honestly say, now that I have found my place in the field of training and development, that every day is exciting. When you find your passion, your job is no longer work. As a matter of fact, once you find it, you will never *work* another day again.

Communication

I graduated from a small four-year Jesuit college. My bachelor's degree is in communication arts, so good communication with a manager is critical to me. I need regular feedback and open communication about expectations.

I don't care what anyone says, being a new and young employee is very exciting (and very frightening.) You are unsure of yourself and of your new environment. This fear can be a real demotivator. Bosses, managers, and supervisors are an intimidating lot. Communicating how I am doing and where I stand is a must for me.

A way to alleviate my fear of the unknown and to keep me motivated is to communicate with me. Give me strokes as much as you can. Strokes are not always positive. As a matter of fact, they can be positive or negative. Regardless of their kind, I need them as often as possible. The worst stroke of all is no stroke at all.

Strokes are any kind of attention you can get from or give to another person. They can be the feedback and communication you give to employees that let them know where they stand, how they are doing, that you, as their manager, acknowledge their existence, and, hopefully, the difference they are making as an employee. Everyone needs strokes. Without them, workers begin filling in the feedback gap, most of the time with their own negative criticism and mental anguish. Positive strokes can be in the form of a thank you, interest, attention, or praise. They make us feel happy, useful, and fulfilled. Negative strokes can be in the form of undue criticism, mistrust, and a lack of gratitude. They can make us feel sad.

Even though I currently work for a boss who travels quite a bit and is often not physically present to give me strokes, he understands their importance to me and that they are a critical motivating factor. When he calls into the office, or leaves me a note, there is usually a stroke. When he is in the office, he greets me in the morning and we spend a few minutes catching up. Often we eat lunch together. Through these efforts, he shows a genuine care and concern for me as a human being.

Expectations

When you assume you know what drives and motivates someone, and you act on those assumptions without ever checking their validity, there is a chance your logic and rationale will fail. Get clear on needs and expectations from the beginning of a working relationship.

I have to share with you an experience I had that illustrates this point. I was sitting on a panel with four other young workers at a major insurance company. Our purpose was to answer questions from the audience of managers about what makes us tick as young workers. I was so taken back by some of the questions, and the fact that not once did anyone in the audience ask us what *we felt we needed* to be successful in a job, or to be productive or motivated. Their questions were all around their already preconceived notions and assumptions of what we needed and wanted, based on what they thought our expectations were in a job. For example, several of the managers got hung up on money and raise issues. "How much of a raise would motivate you to be productive?" "What percentage of a raise would keep you satisfied at your six-months review?" I became so frustrated by these questions. Where did these managers even get the notion that money would motivate us in the first place? The problem was that these managers never stopped to cross-check if their perceptions of our expectations were accurate. They were in the midst of setting policies around raise and money issues in hope of motivating their young workers to a higher level, without ever

183

having checked to see if money and raises were a key motivating factor for us in the first place. It was as if these managers were trying to build the better mousetrap for young workers without first asking if we had mice.

When managers and workers communicate their needs and expectations, the guesswork is removed and you're on your way to a win-win relationship. When needs and expectations start to change, when they are no longer getting met, communicate. To me, open communication around needs and expectations is one of the most important aspects of a manager-employee relationship.

Money, Materialism, and More

Speaking of money issues, as I spend more time in the business world, I am beginning to realize that many managers believe my generation is very motivated monetarily. Well, as for me, money is important, and I definitely want enough to live on and to occasionally afford nice things for myself. But money is not one of my chief motivating factors in a job. I believe salary is not a job motivator, it is part of a contract for work. In exchange for duties performed, you will receive this amount of money every two weeks. I do expect salary reviews and raises. I do expect to be compensated well for the work that I perform and the value and contribution I add to my company. But this is a basic expectation for any employee, almost a basic requirement. It does not add value to my job and will not motivate me to a higher level. It is not seen as appreciation for a job well done or for having gone above and beyond the call of duty.

If you want to add value to my job and motivate me to a higher level, here are some perks that I have received in the past which have motivated me, increased my commitment to my job, and increased my productivity:

I have enjoyed the benefit of a couple of "free days" from work—a reward for overtime I put in on a particular project. They did not count as vacation days, or sick time, but free time for having gone the extra mile to finish a project. Will I be inclined to go the extra mile the next time I am needed? Count on it! I have also received rewards such as a weekend at a hotel for myself and my husband, cash bonuses, and dinners and lunches with both my boss and the president of my company.

However, not all rewards have to cost the company money in order to motivate me; I have also enjoyed the opportunity to attend executive meetings, sales calls with a senior staff member, and even to spend a full day with my boss doing his job alongside him, including attending meetings and having lunch together. Of course, these ideas still may cost the company *something,* but there are ways to motivate me that don't cost a penny and are greatly appreciated. My favorite are the Post-it notes that I receive occasionally on my paycheck saying, "Thanks for all your hard work" or "I really appreciate all you do for me." These notes thrill me. They are personal, from the heart, and really make me feel appreciated for who I am and my unique contribution to my company. They motivate me and have a lasting effect. I stick them up on my refrigerator so that I can read them every morning before I go to work.

Performance Reviews
My first performance review kept me awake at night for weeks, pondering my fate. I had never had a performance review in my life. Sure I had grades, but they were measurable and based on tangible products: reports, tests, class attendance. But this was different. How was my performance going to be judged? What if my boss just decided he didn't like me anymore? What if I had failed? What if he were to fire me? The more I thought about the fated day, the more wound up and upset I got, and the more my imagination ran wild.

I walked into my first review shaking and with, I'm sure, very bloodshot eyes. No, I did not drug myself to get through the review, I just hadn't slept in weeks, remember? Well, I walked in with my pencil and paper, and a medal of Saint Jude (patron saint of hopeless causes and things despaired of) clenched tightly in my hand. My boss greeted me with a big smile and said, "Come on, let's have some breakfast as we talk." We ate at one of my favorite restaurants and talked about my goals, my evaluation of myself, my job, and his feedback. It went very well! Even though he had some constructive criticism, I was open to it because of the environment he created, and the mood he set for the review. All those needless nights without sleep!

The lesson? My boss did not realize that this was my first performance review, and I never told him. So I went through a great deal of anxiety about this review because I really did not understand its goals or purpose. Of course, I had heard the horror stories around "reviews" and "evaluations." I guess I started to believe them. So I encourage you, as a manager, to talk with your young workers about reviews. Ask your employees what their perceptions of performance reviews are. Tell them exactly what your goals are for the review, what they will be reviewed upon, and what you would like your young workers to prepare in advance. Relieve their anxiety as best you can. Remember, perhaps, like me, they won't admit that they have never been reviewed before.

Lead and I Will Follow

What I have appreciated the most in past relationships with bosses and managers is having an ability to work together. Their ability to lead me, and my willingness to follow through the mutual trust and respect came from what we had built for one another. Douglas Stewart contends that "the power to lead really flows upward from those who are being led."[1]

He describes how organizations have shifted from managing things to leading people. No longer are the biggest assets of companies tangible goods; their biggest assets now are their people. Stewart notes that "people cannot be successfully managed in the same way as things." He argues that in this shift the traditional push-oriented authority-manager has given way to the new pull-oriented leader-manager. This example shows the distinction between "push-oriented" and "pull-oriented":

In automobiles, it is the difference between front-wheel drive (pulling) or rear-wheel drive (pushing). And when the going gets slippery or tough, there's no question that front-wheel drive is much more likely to get you to your destination. Think of your own preference when you've been in tough situations: did you want someone leaning and pushing on your backside, or putting out a hand to help pull you out of the difficulties? Your employees are no different.[2]

In Warren Bennis's opinion, "The problem with many organizations, and especially the ones that are failing, is that they tend to be overmanaged and underled."[3] My guess is that my generation will respond most favorably to the front-wheel pull of a leader-manager. This leadership style is definitely my preference.

The following chart (page 188) reflects the influence of these management styles on workers. Here are some descriptions of the differences between these styles.

Stewart states the "Do as I say because I said it" approach is increasingly less viable with modern employees.

What Is Ageism?

The Gray Panthers, a nonprofit organization made up of people of all ages who advocate many human rights issues, say ageism is

age-related discrimination, which is illegal in our country: Ageism is discrimination or stereotyping based on age. It is as destructive of persons as racism and sexism, and equally pervasive in our society. Ageism is most evident with the elderly, but is present in all age groups. The 40-year-old who is told she is too old for a job, the 18-year-old whose opinions are disregarded because of his inexperience, or the child whose life is completely controlled by her parents are all victims of ageism.[4]

Many times I have felt it. Many times I have been guilty of it myself; but I never fully understood ageism until now. I can honestly say that not a day goes by when I don't wish I were thir-

Authority-manager   *Leader-managers*[5]

Traits and Methods:

Authority-based	Influence-based
Position power	Personal power
Tell-oriented	Ask-oriented
Retains authority	Shares authority
Defines limits	Expands limits
Enforces	Reinforces
Restricts creativity	Encourages creativity
One-way communication	Two-way communication
Personal distance	Personal interest
Mandates	Persuades
Dictates	Sells
Task orientation	Human resource orientation
Arbitrates	Negotiates
Requires loyalty	Obtains commitment

Which Result in:

Dependency	Interdependency
Reluctant production	Voluntary performance
Compliance	Commitment
"Crisis" problem-solving	"Prevention" problem-solving
Stress	Challenge
Malicious obedience	Creative performance
Discouragement	Empowerment

Reprinted by permission of John Wiley and Sons, Inc.

tysomething. My friends who are older always say in response, "You're crazy to wish you were older," or "Why wish your life away? It's hell to be thirtysomething or worse yet, fortysomething," or "Being young is a time to have fun, discover things, pursue your dreams." Well, I'll tell you what being twentysomething is all about. It is hard as hell. Constantly being told, "You are too young to do this or to do that." Of course, right along with being too young, most of the time in the same breath is, "You don't have enough experience." The catch-22 in all of this is, "You are too young for me to take a risk with you and give you the experience you need." So how is it that being young is a time to discover things and pursue your dreams when you can't get the experience to do it? This is ageism. Are you guilty of it?

Many managers say to younger workers, "I'll do it myself. After all, I've been here twenty-five years and I know how it is supposed to be done." For many managers, twenty-five years' experience with a company just means you've lived the same year over 25 times. It just doesn't hold much weight with me or my peers. Actions speak louder than words. If you want me to step aside and let you carry out one of my responsibilities for me because you are afraid I won't do it correctly, then be prepared to impress the hell out of me. Prove to me that you were right, that you can perform the task better. Then be prepared to show me how to do it the right way so I walk away from the experience having learned something. If you don't, your credibility with me is shot. Don't expect much respect from me from that point on.

The advice that the Gray Panthers provide to people for combating ageism is:

- Think and talk about yourself in a positive way.
- Accept honest compliments without embarrassment.
- Insist on fair treatment.
- Keep well informed about social and political issues.[6]

These are good words to live by when you are twentysomething, or any age.

Those Cynical Youth

I have some insight to why so many people refer to my generation as cynical. We are always questioning authority, asking why. Here is my insight. I am virtually as unimpressed with older generations as you are with my generation. Where is the magic? I have watched politicians engage in dirty politics and mud-slinging. I have watched countries enslave their people, limit their freedoms, create social unrest. I have inherited a planet that is terribly polluted, with people who believe everything is expendable, even other people. Here is an Earth running short of everything precious: water, clean air, healthy children, trees, free space, forests, and plains.

We have a population of parents who abuse their children; then, when their children turn to drugs and street gangs to try to fill an empty and aching heart, they look at the children in disgust and say, "What is wrong with them? Aren't they just awful? We weren't like that." Yet, we are the group of people getting all of the criticism for being cynical. I think Layne Longfellow's comment bears repeating: "The way I see the world is the result of the world that I have seen."[7]

Out There

I have often heard my generation referred to as the "me" generation. What this label implies to me is that we are all self-centered, so much so that we rarely acknowledge anything in our world that doesn't pertain immediately and directly to ourselves and our future. I disagree with this label for my generation. Perhaps it fits some of my peers; some are very "me" centered. But I bet it describes many people in your generation, in all generations as well. Self-centeredness is not unique to my generation. Writing this chapter, I remember hearing news of the Persian Gulf War on the radio in the background. Thousands of people, many my age, were facing the reality of death in a desert half a world away from me. They went without hesitation for this country. They are the same individuals referred to in so many tabloids as "me-centered, only interested in money and personal gain, only interested in what's in it for me." I guess by going bravely, proudly, and without hesitation to war, we didn't quite live up to this reputation, did we?

The important thing is that managers need to acknowledge that "whole people" are working for them—whole people with feelings, emotions, and opinions. Don't assume that your young workers are not aware of world events; don't assume that events make no difference to them personally and professionally.

Last Words

Managers have a responsibility to make informed decisions about their departments and their employees, whatever those decisions may be. The biggest mistake would be to make uninformed choices on how to manage your young workers—choices based on what you think we need, and not based on the facts of who we are as individuals.

Don't clump us together. Don't label us. Particularly, please don't label us all the "me generation." We aren't all alike. We are people first, young workers second. There is much strength in our differences. Maybe the only thing we all do have in common is our age. Incorrect perceptions and broad generalizations about us drive us nuts. When these incorrect perceptions are acted upon and sweeping management policies based on these generalizations are executed, it leads to immediate failure.

Maybe the best management policy in the world is one that is particular and unique to each of the individuals being managed. Maybe there should be as many management styles and policies as there are people to manage.

TAKING ACTION

- *Begin getting to know your young workers as individuals by asking the following questions:*

  1. Tell me about yourself: Where did you grow up, and where did you go to school?
  2. What types of managers or teachers have you had in the past? Describe what you liked and did not like about the way they worked with you.
  3. What is important to you in a relationship with a manager or supervisor?
  4. What is important to you in a relationship with a coworker?
  5. How do you like to be rewarded for your work? For a job well done?
  6. Have you ever been reviewed, either formally or informally, at a job before?
  7. What is the best way for us to communicate with each other when we need to discuss a problem or resolve a conflict?

- *The next step is to share about yourself, as a manager or supervisor, with your young worker.*

  1. This is how I like to work with my employees.
  2. These are my expectations.
  3. This is how I am used to reviewing employees.
  4. Here are some ways that I use to communicate with the people who work for me.
  5. This is the management style I use most often and that is comfortable to me. How does it sound to you? Is there something different that you need from me, as your manager, to succeed at this job?

CHAPTER-AT-A-GLANCE

- Get to know your young workers as unique individuals. Information and knowledge about twentysomethings will help you understand and lead them successfully.

- Young workers' expectations are shaped by past experiences, including how they were reared, where they went to school, and other jobs they've held.

- Get clear on the expectations you have of twentysomething workers and understand the expectations they have of you and the job.

- Remember that many experiences on the job will be new to the young worker, for example, performance reviews. Explain the experiences and use some patience while your young worker adjusts to them.

- Twentysomethings need feedback and communication from their manager about how they're doing. They may have been deprived of time and attention from their parents. Give lots of positive strokes. The worst stroke is no stroke.

- Business school graduates are savvy about management styles. They may expect a more progressive management style from you, such as coaching and counseling, instead of traditional push-oriented management.

- Prevent ageism, and help others in your organization put their age biases aside.

- Be flexible in your leadership style.

Notes

1. Douglas Stewart, *The Power of People Skills,* A Wiley Press Book, John Wiley and Sons, Inc., 1986, pp. 172, 173.
2. Ibid.
3. Warren Bennis and Burt Nanus, *Leaders: Strategies for Taking Charge,* Harper and Row, 1985, quoted in Douglas Stewart, *The Power of People Skills,* p. 171.

4. Gray Panthers of Austin, Texas, and Denver, Colorado.
5. Stewart.
6. Ibid.
7. Layne A. Longfellow, "Ethics to Excellence; the Route to Productivity," presentation at Clearwater Beach, Florida, April 2, 1989.

It's time for the baby bust to bust loose.

—Claire Raines

12

It's Up to You

You've got all the pieces of the puzzle now. You've explored the demographics of the twentysomething generation and delved into their attitudes—about work and bosses, about themselves and others. You know more now about how they see the world and how they respond to authority. You've read case studies and interviews with twentysomethings and some of the folks who supervise them. You've examined their values and how they got them. You've read about the shifting economy and increasingly diverse workforce. You've worried along with us about what can be done to handle the skills shortfall. You've looked into the challenges facing the young supervisor.

Those are the jigsaw pieces we've provided. Now it's time to put the puzzle together. It's up to you.

We'd like to share a story our friend Jim Hunt heard recently in England.

> There once was a teacher who had worked long and hard with a particularly outstanding student on a major geography project. Together, the student and teacher went through maps and geography books, atlases, and globes. For months, they worked in textbooks about climate, mapping, and navigation. Now it was time for the final task. The teacher wanted to make sure the student's last assignment would challenge him completely, requiring him to call upon all his resources, knowledge, skills, and commitment.

So she took a large paper map of the world and tore it into hundreds of tiny pieces. Then she laid it on the table in front of him, explaining that his final task was to put the map back together. Thinking this job would take him a few hours, she left the room.

A half-hour later, she returned. To her astonishment, the student was seated—with every piece of the puzzle in place on the table in front of him.

She spoke softly. "I wasn't even sure it was possible to complete this task. But I thought, if you could do it, it surely would take hours. Do you mind if I ask: how did you do this?"

He seemed rather thoughtful. "Well," he said, "like you, I wasn't certain it could be done. I was overwhelmed when you left. All those little pieces. How could I—just one person—get all of that put together? Then I discovered the something that made the difference. I discovered that on the back of the map was a picture of a person. And I found that once I put the person together, the rest would follow."

You are the leader. We invite you to put your energies into yourself—into constantly updating and improving your coaching skills, your knowledge base, your sensitivity, your communication skills. Look for that young person in the puzzle. Then the rest will follow.

The twentysomething generation will achieve great things with leaders like you.

196

About the Authors

Lawrence J. Bradford, Ph.D. is the founder of *Inner-Change*™ *Seminars.* He works with companies throughout the United States to help them manage organizational change and improve the performance of individuals. A professional speaker and trainer, Larry is recognized as one of the country's leading experts in making superior customer service the driving force of any business. He is the co-author of *The Service Advantage: How to Identify and Fulfill Customer Needs.* For information on consulting or training events, call (303) 670-2755, or write to *Inner-Change*™ *Seminars,* 7854 Armadillo Trail, Evergreen, CO 80439.

Claire Raines, M.A. is considered one of the nation's leading experts on Generation X. A dynamic speaker, Claire has received rave reviews for her keynote speeches which help audiences better understand the generations. Her presentations offer thought-provoking facts, engaging anecdotes, and practical applications. Claire has been featured widely in the media, including *USA Today, Training Magazine, Working Woman,* and *Personnel Journal.* In her consulting practice, she works with companies to provide the tools for understanding young workers. For availability and fee arrangements, please contact Jaclyn Yelich at (303) 399-0630.

To Order Additional Copies

To order **less than ten** copies of *Twentysomething: Managing and Motivating Today's New Work Force,* please call:
The Tattered Cover Bookstore
(800) 833-9327
(303) 322-7727

To order **ten or more copies**, please call:

Lawrence J. Bradford   or   Claire Raines
(303) 670-2755   (303) 322-0474

Index

Achiever value system, 44–45, 134, 142
Adams, Ken, 43, 45
Adolescence, extended, 35
Adolph Coors Company, 35, 41
Advancement, attitude toward, 6
Aetna Life and Casualty, 64
African-Americans in the work force, 52, 55–56
Ageism, 187–89
American Council on Education, 41
American Freshman: Twenty Year Trends, 32
American Productivity Center, 172
ARC International, 115, 125
Asian-Americans in the work force, 52, 57–59
Astin, Alexander, 36
Authority, attitude toward, 6, 12–13, 37, 111–13, 189–90

Baby boomers, 7, 9, 38, 104–6
Basic skills deficit, 3–4, 54–56, 69–73, 82
Ben & Jerry's, 116–17
Beneficial Corporation, 80–81
Bennis, Warren, 187
Bernhardt, Kenneth, 34
Book of Questions, The, 48
Boyer, Jeanne, 75
Brain Technologies Corporation, 43

Bridges, William, 147
Burger King, 76

"Can This Marriage Be Saved?" 20
Careers, 7–8, 174
   seven phases of development, 107–110
Case studies and examples
   education gap, narrowing, 74–77, 80
   interviews of managers, 85, 91–97
   interviews of twentysomethings, 85–91, 177–92
   managing twentysomething employees, 20–29, 116–18
   minorities and women in the work force, 62–64
   seasonal workers, 167–71
   values and matching leadership styles, 127–41
Catalyst, Inc., 59
Cavazos, Laura, 68
Chain of command, 12–13, 111–13
Chesterton, G.K., 114
Choice-seeker value system, 45, 140, 143
Chrysler Corporation, 68, 74, 81, 112
Coaching, 114, 119–20, 126
Cohen, Ben, 116
College graduates, 4, 58–59, 68
Colorado Mountain College, 167
Commitment, slowness with, 36–37

Conflict confrontation skills, 156–57
Contemporary magazine, 71
Contracts, 13, 25, 120–21
  Personal Performance Contracts, 121
Corning Glass, 74
Corroon and Black Corporation, 165, 173–74
Crisp Publications, 80–81
Crites, Richard, 75
Cynicism, 32, 189–90

Dalkemper, Leslie, 47
Daniels, Bill, 46
Decision-making, 6, 113–14, 186–87
Delayering, 112
DeLoalich, Eugene, 56
DePree, Max, 127
Development, 77–78
Disneyland and Disney World, 27, 169–71
"Don't Worry, Be Happy," 14
Drucker, Peter, 110
Dylan, Bob, 53–54

Earnings, attitude toward, 6, 34, 184–85
Economy, shifting, 53–55
Education, 68–82
  apprenticeships and internships, 76–77
  at the workplace, 68, 74–82
  basic skills deficit, 3–4, 54–56, 69–73, 82
  blame, placing, 70–72
  High school dropouts, 4, 56–57
  higher level demanded by new jobs, 4, 68, 73–74
  higher level of twentysomething workers, 4, 146
  hiring instructors, 79–81

humanities, need for course work in, 71
international perspective, 76–77
temporary and seasonal workers, 170–71, 173
see also Training
Empowering employees, 114–15, 126
Entry-level positions, 4, 54
Essence, 56
Expectancy, theory of, 171–72

Farnsworth, Martha, 35
Feedback, 25–26, 29
Feminist movement, 60
Flexibility in schedules, 8, 27
Fordham University, 42
Ford Motor Company, 7, 112
Fortune magazine, 7–8, 52
Friends, supervising, 150
Fritz, Roger, 121
Fun, attitude toward, 14–15, 26, 27, 29, 36, 107

General Motors Corporation, 112
Generational values model (MindMaker6), 31, 43–46, 65, 133–34, 142
Generations, differences between, 103–7, 110
Georgia State University, 34
Germany, apprenticeship programs in, 76–77
Graves, Clare, 43
Gray Panthers, 187–89
Great Britain, closing skills gap in, 77
Greenfield, Jerry, 116

Haas, Robert D., 62
Halperin, Samuel, 4
Harvard Business Review, 59, 62
Healy, Jane, 71

Hewlett-Packard, 35–36, 43
Hierarchy, management, 12–13, 111–13
Higher Education Research Institute (UCLA), 32–34, 36
High school seniors, values of, 5–6
Hill, Bill, 167–68, 171–72
Hirsch, Paul, 40
Hispanics in the work force, 52, 56–57
Hunt, Jim, 195

Iacocca, Lee, 74, 81
Immigration and the work force, 55
Index of Social Health for Children and Youth, 42
Institute for Social Research, University of Michigan, 5
Interviews
    format, 98–99
    of managers, 85, 91–97
    of twentysomethings, 85–91, 177–92
Involver value system, 45, 137, 143

Jackson, Jesse, 52
Japanese "kaizen" management theory, 174
Job security, attitude toward, 6–8, 15
Johnson & Johnson Corporation, 165

KCFR radio station, 47
Keck, Mahin & Cate, 165
Kennedy, John F., assassination of, 33
Kinsperson value system, 43, 138, 142

Labor force
    delayed entry, 69–70
    shrinking, 3, 40–41, 102
Ladies Home Journal, 20

Large corporations, interest in working for, 5–6
Latchkey children, 14, 40, 178–80
Leadership Is an Art, 127
Leadership styles and strategies
    adapting to twentysomething generation, 27, 46, 61, 106–7, 110–16, 124, 127
    based on worker values, 134–43
    coaching, 114, 119–20, 126
    examples, 116–18, 127–41, 186–87.
    individualizing, 124–43, 191–92
    key principles, 125–26
    organization chart differences, 111–13
    twenty-first century, 113–16, 124–43
"Leave It to Beaver," 14, 40
Leisure time, 8
LensCrafters, 63
Letter to a Manager, 177–92
Levi Strauss Corporation, 62–63
Lewis, Edward, 56
L.L. Bean, 165
Loner value system, 43–44, 139, 142
Longfellow, Layne A., 5, 39, 42, 190
Loyalist value system, 44, 136, 142

Maccoby, Michael, 12–13
Managers
    adjustments, need for, 14, 27, 46, 61, 106–7, 110–16, 124, 127
    baby boomers, 7, 9, 38, 104–6
    confidence in, 112–13
    front-line, 111
    letter to, 177–92
    parenting, 24, 26, 29
    perceptions about twentysomething work force, 1–2, 103–10
    supervisors, 111, 113–14
    traditionalists, 7, 38, 104–6

Managers *(cont'd)*
  understanding of
    twentysomethings, increasing,
    17, 48–49, 125, 192
  values of, as contrasted with
    twentysomething values, 7, 9,
    20–29, 38, 104–6
Manufacturing, 53–54
Marriage, attitude toward, 15
Marriott Corporation, 63–64
Massey, Morris, 39
Materialism, 34–35, 184–85
McArthur, Connie, 74–75
McBride, Bob, 41
McDonald's, 117–18
Minorities in the work force,
  demographics, 52, 56–60, 65
  economic shift, 53–55
  immigration, 55
Miringoff, Marc, 42
Money, attitude toward, 6, 34,
  184–85
Morgan State University, 56
"Mother's Work," 61

National Science Foundation, 69
NBC/United Airlines *In-Flight
  Report,* 76
Neifert, Larry, 107
Newsweek magazine, 33

Older or more experienced
  employees, supervising, 153–55
Open door policy, 65
Organization chart, 111–12
Orienting new employees, 25, 29,
  115–16
  Disneyland example, 170–71

Paradigm shifts, 53, 110, 112, 114
Parents of twentysomethings
  description, 39–40, 71
  example, 178–80

managers as, 24, 26, 29
older employees as, 154–55
television as surrogate, 9, 14, 42,
  71
Part-time workers, 165–66. *See also*
  Temporary and seasonal
  workers
Persian Gulf War, 8, 33, 38, 42, 53,
  56, 125, 190
Persico, Linda, 7
Personal Performance Contracts,
  121
Peter Hart Research Associates, 33
Peters, Tom, 126
Pizza Hut, 73
Platinum Rule, 114
Plurality training, 65
Powell, Colin, 55
Power of People Skills, The, 178
Praise, 107, 173
Promotion, attitude toward, 6
Public Service Company of
  Colorado, 74–75, 81

Quality of life, importance of, 7
Quid pro quo attitude, 13

Rainbow coalition, 52–53. *See
  also* Minorities in the work
  force
Raines, Claire, 107
Reagan, Ronald, 9, 42
Recognition, importance of, 107,
  185–86
Regan, Margaret, 7
Reich, Robert, 71
Reinemund, Steve, 73
Resistant employees, supervising,
  155–57
Risk taking, attitude toward, 9

Samon, Katherine Ann, 12
Schwartz, Felice N., 59

Selleck, Tom, 120
Service occupations, 53–54
Seventeen magazine, 41
Siemens Corporation, 76
Society, attitude toward, 6, 8–9, 32, 46–47, 190
Status, attitude toward, 6, 34
Stewart, Douglas, 178, 186
Stone, Nan, 61
Stress, 42
Supervisors, twentysomething
  actions to take, 162–63
  encouraging self-confidence in, 145–63
  friends, 150–53
  mentoring, 160–61
  mistake management, 158–60
  older or more experienced employees, 153–55
  resistant employees, 155–57
  transition to supervision, 147–50
  younger employees, 157–58
Surviving Corporate Transition, 147
Sweden, closing skills gap in, 77

Tanelian, Katherine, 3, 5–6
Television, 9, 14, 42, 71
Temporary and seasonal workers, 165–74
  actions to take, 173–74
  case studies, 167–71
  demographics, 165
  motivating, 167–71
  problems with, 166–67
  theory of expectancy, 171–72
Three Men and a Baby, 120
Thriving on Chaos, 126
Time magazine, 8, 42
Time spent with managers, importance of, 26, 29, 36, 107, 185
Traditionalists, 7, 38, 104–6

Training
  apprenticeships and internships, 76–77
  at the workplace, 68, 74–82
  definition, 77–78
  expert help in, 79–81
  gap, 3–4, 54–56, 69–73, 82
  needs analysis, 78–79
  temporary and seasonal workers, 170–71, 173
  see also Education
Transition
  difference from change, 147–48
  phases of, 148–50
Twenty-five-year-olds, values of, 7–8
Twentysomething generation
  attracting and keeping, 3, 102
  characteristics, 2–17
  complaints about, 1–2, 103–10
  demographics, 3, 40–41, 102
  exceptions among, 15, 191
  influences that shaped, 39–42
  job search example, 180–82
  understanding, 17, 48–49, 125, 192.
"Two-minute mind," 71

UCLA Higher Education Research Institute survey, 32–34, 36
University of Denver, 46–47
University of Michigan, Institute for Social Research, 5
University of Texas, 69
USA Today, 38
U.S. Department of Education, 69
U.S. News and World Report, 68, 70
U.S. West Corporation, 74–75, 81

Wall Street Journal, 9
Watergate, 39, 42
White, Robert, 114
Wilder, Douglas, 55
William T. Grant Foundation, 4

Women in the work force, 52–65
   demographics, 59–60
   examples, 62–64
   flexibility, need for, 61
Women's movement, 60
Work, attitude toward, 5–8, 173
Workforce America, 52

Working Woman magazine, 12
World War II-era managers, 7, 38,
   104–6

Yellow sneaker syndrome, 145–46
Yiffies, 8
Younker, John, 172